FOLK-STYLE GUITAR

FOLK-STYLE GUITAR

By Harry Taussig

Oak Publications, New York
Music Sales Limited, London

Book design by Carol Freeman

Copyright © 1973 by Oak Publications,
A Division of Embassy Music Corporation, New York, NY.

All rights reserved. No part of this book may be
reproduced in any form or by any electronic or mechanical means
including information storage and retrieval systems,
without permission in writing from the publisher
except by a reviewer who may quote brief passages in a review.

Order No. OK 62612
International Standard Book Number: 0.8256.0136.3
Library of Congress Catalog Card Number: 72-76830

Exclusive Distributors:
Music Sales Corporation
257 Park Avenue South, New York, NY 10010 USA
Music Sales Limited
8/9 Frith Street, London W1V 5TZ England
Music Sales Pty. Limited
120 Rothschild Street, Rosebery, Sydney, NSW 2018, Australia

Printed in the United States of America by
Vicks Lithograph and Printing Corporation

CONTENTS

- 7 Foreword
- 8 Introduction
- 12 The Basic Guitar Keys
  - 12 Oh, Susanna—Key of G
  - 13 *Oh, Susanna—Solo*
  - 15 Jesse James—Carter-Style Picking in the Key of G
  - 16 *Jesse James—Solo*
  - 18 *Jesse James—Melody*
  - 20 Little Maggie—The D Chord
    Little Maggie—Solo
  - 21 *Little Maggie—Melody*
  - 22 I Never Will Marry—Key of D
  - 23 *I Never Will Marry—Solo*
  - 24 *I Never Will Marry—Melody*
    Railroad Bill—The E and E7 Chords
  - 26 *Railroad Bill—Solo*
  - 27 *Railroad Bill—Melody*
  - 28 John Hardy—Key of A
    John Hardy—Solo
  - 30 *John Hardy—Melody*
  - 31 Red River Valley—More Key of A
  - 33 *Red River Valley—Solo*
  - 34 *Red River Valley—Melody*
  - 35 Little Rosewood Casket—The Long A Chord
  - 36 *Little Rosewood Casket—Solo*
  - 37 *Little Rosewood Casket—Melody*
  - 38 Banks of the Ohio—Long A in the Key of D
  - 39 *Banks of the Ohio—Solo*
  - 40 *Banks of the Ohio—Melody*
  - 41 Sugar Babe—Key of E
    Sugar Babe—Solo
    Summary
- 42 More Chords
  - 42 The Great Silkie
    The Great Silkie—Solo
  - 43 *The Great Silkie—Melody*
  - 44 Acres of Clams—The Am Chord
    Acres of Clams—Solo
  - 46 *Acres of Clams—Melody*
  - 48 Columbus Stockade Blues—More Am Chords
    Columbus Stockade Blues—Solo
  - 50 *Columbus Stockade Blues—Melody*
  - 52 House of the Rising Sun
    House of the Rising Sun—Solo
  - 53 *House of the Rising Sun—Melody*
  - 54 Cruel War Is Raging—Fingerpicking Am Chords
  - 56 *Cruel War Is Raging—Solo*
  - 57 *Cruel War Is Raging—Melody*
  - 58 Scarborough Fair—The Dm Chord
  - 59 *Scarborough Fair—Solo*
  - 60 *Scarborough Fair—Melody*
  - 62 Railroad Bill—A New G7 Chord
  - 63 *Railroad Bill—Solo*
  - 64 Bully of the Town
  - 66 *Bully of the Town—Solo*
- 68 Hammers and Slides
  - 68 Stackerlee—Simple Hammers
  - 71 *Stackerlee—Solo*
  - 72 *Stackerlee—Melody*
  - 73 Railroad Bill #2—Off-Beat Hammers
  - 74 *Railroad Bill #2—Solo*
  - 75 Tom Dooley—Hammers in C and G
  - 77 *Tom Dooley—Solo*

78	Freight Train—Hammers in F	101	*Railroad Bill #3—Solo*
80	*Freight Train—Solo*	102	Oh, Mary, Don't You Weep #2—Hammers and Picks
81	*Freight Train—Melody*	103	*Oh, Mary, Don't You Weep #2—Solo*
82	Freight Train #2—The Real Thing	104	Casey Jones—Key of G
83	*Freight Train #2—Solo*	105	*Casey Jones—Solo*
84	One Dime Blues—Slides	106	Frankie and Johnny—Key of A
86	*One Dime Blues—Solo*		*Frankie and Johnny—Solo*
87	*One Dime Blues—Melody*	107	*Frankie and Johnny—Melody*
88	Salty Dog—Combined Hammers and Slides	108	Sugar Babe—More Hammers
	Salty Dog—Solo		*Sugar Babe—Solo*
89	*Salty Dog—Melody*	109	Midnight Special—Complex Three-Finger Picking
90	Salty Dog #2—Complex Hammers and Slides	111	*Midnight Special—Solo*
92	*Salty Dog #2—Solo*	112	*Midnight Special—Melody*
	Salty Dog #2—Melody		
93	See See Rider—Off-Beat Slides and Picks	114	Doing It All Yourself
94	*See See Rider—Solo*	115	*Bury Me Beneath The Willow*
96	*See See Rider—Melody*	116	*The Girl on the Greenbriar Shore*
		117	*Handsome Molly*
97	Three-Finger Picking	118	*Oh, Babe, It Ain't No Lie*
97	Oh, Mary, Don't You Weep—Three-Finger Picking	119	*East Virginia Blues*
	Oh, Mary, Don't You Weep—Solo	120	*Tom Cat Blues*
98	*Oh, Mary, Don't You Weep—Melody*	121	*Nine-Pound Hammer*
99	Hush, Little Baby—New Right-Hand Position	122	*Just A Closer Walk With Thee*
	Hush, Little Baby—Solo	123	*Camptown Races*
100	*Hush, Little Baby—Melody*	124	*Swanee River*
	Railroad Bill #3—Hammers	125	*Sinner Man*
		126	*Keep Your Lamp Trimmed and Burning*

FOREWORD

The intent of this book is to illustrate the basic techniques of finger-style guitar playing. Beginning with the most elementary forms of finger-picking, this book concentrates on developing guitar skills and dexterity. It assumes that some facility has already been acquired—the appropriate background material can be obtained from *Teach Yourself Guitar* (Oak Publications).

While the melodies and text to many of the songs are included, the emphasis is on the instrumental solo. The musical examples are devised to illustrate specific points and techniques and have been carefully graded in difficulty. Each example introduces only one or two new items or techniques and can be easily assimilated into one's repertoire. For these reasons this book may be used with or without an instructor.

I hope everyone who ventures into guitar playing with this book derives as much pleasure from traditional American music as I have over the past years.

INTRODUCTION

The purpose of this introduction is to familiarize the intermediate guitar student with specific formal notations used. If you feel that the material is too difficult, please take this opportunity to study *Teach Yourself Guitar* (Oak Publications). This will lead you smoothly into the material presented in this book.

In order to represent chords we need some sort of shorthand notation. In figure A, we show a sketch of a guitar on the left and what we call a chord diagram on the right. The chord diagram is simply a schematic view of a portion of the guitar as seen from the top. We use the chord diagram to show where we put our fingers on the guitar. Notice that the first string, or the highest pitched string, is to the right in the diagram and the lowest pitched string is on the left.

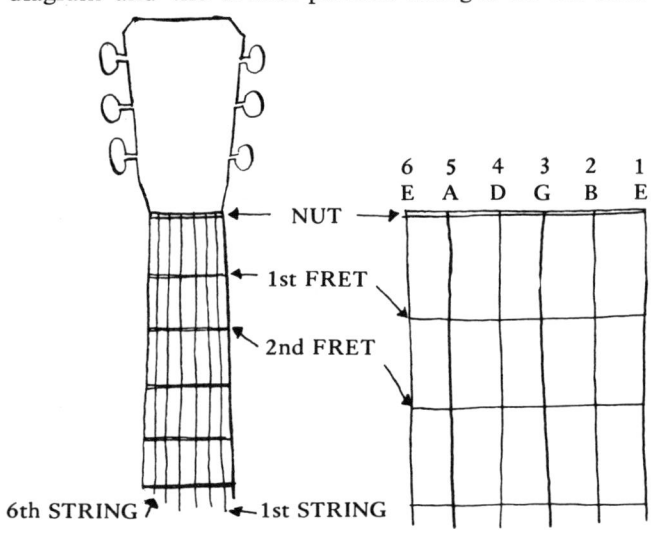

Figure A

Thus we see that the vertical lines represent the strings and the horizontal lines represent the frets of the guitar. (Frets are the metal inserts on the guitar neck perpendicular to the strings.)

The place where fingers are to be positioned are indicated by black dots. From the chord diagram and the sketch, we see that for the C chord the index finger frets the second string at the first fret, the second finger frets the fourth string at the second fret, and the third finger frets the fifth string at the third fret:

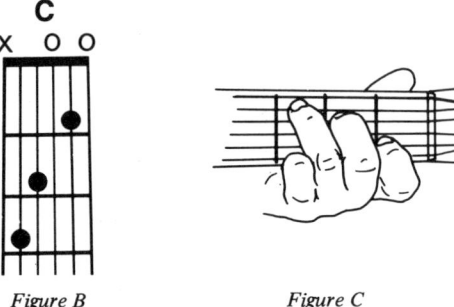

Figure B   *Figure C*

Notice the C above the chord diagram. This indicates that this is the complete C chord. Also notice the little "x" above the sixth string. This means that this string is not used in the chord and should not be sounded.

The "o" indicates that the string is to be sounded open, that is, unfretted.

Before beginning, we should be familiar with two more chords. The first of these is the G7 chord and the second is the F chord. When two strings are

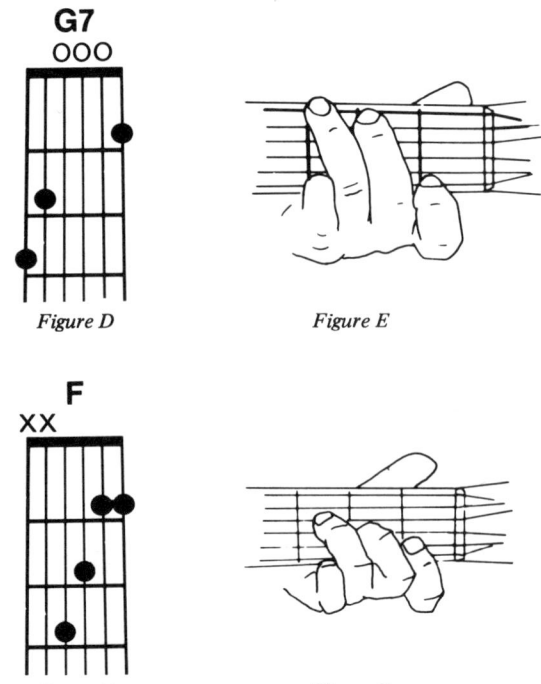

Figure D   *Figure E*

Figure F   *Figure G*

fretted with the same finger, the dots in the chord diagram are connected by a curved line as in the F chord. The three chords, C, F and G7 form principle chords in the key of C. You should be familiar with the key of C before beginning the first chapter of this book.

The most common supplementary notation used in guitar instruction books is tablature.

The six horizontal lines of the tablature, as shown in Figure H, represent the six strings of the guitar. The highest pitched, the first string, corresponds to the top line of the tablature. The second string is represented by the second line. Similarly for the other strings.

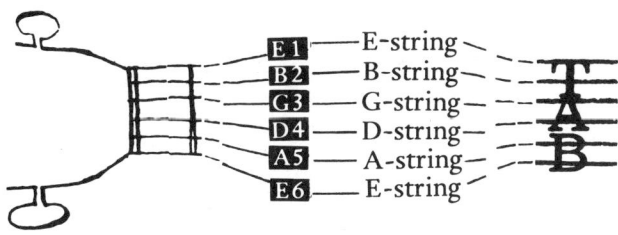

Figure H

Now that we have a method of indicating which strings are to be played, we need a way of indicating the frets. We can number the frets in the following way: zero corresponds to an open string, one corresponds to a string fretted at the first fret, etc. We can write the fret number to be played on the string (or line) to be played in the tablature.

By using the rules for tablature, let us decipher the tablature shown in Figure I. The capital TAB means we are reading tablature (and not music). The

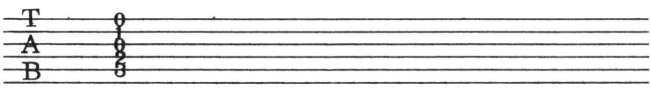

Figure I

uppermost line (corresponding to the first string) has a zero written on it, thus the first string is to be sounded open, i.e., not fretted. The second line has a number one on it indicating that the second string is to be fretted at the first fret. The zero on the third line shows the third string to be sounded open. The fourth string is stopped at the second fret and the fifth string at the third fret. The sixth string is not to be played since nothing is indicated on it. If you will hold down all the indicated notes at one time you will find that this corresponds to a C chord—which we already know.

Since all the numerals in the tablature are written in a vertical row, they are all to be sounded at the same time. Tablature, as normal writing, is read serially from left to right.

Both tablature and music are divided into rhythmic units by vertical lines called *bars* or *bar lines*. The divisions produced by the bar lines are called *measures*.

The two numbers at the beginning of the music and tablature are called the *time signature* which indicates the total time value of each measure. Thus, if all the time were added up it must equal the value indicated by the time signature for each measure.

The lower number of the time signature tells the time value of each beat or count. The quarter note will be used as the rhythmic unit for most of the music in this book. Unless otherwise specified you can take a quarter note to be equal to one beat.

The upper number of the time signature indicates the number of such counts or beats per measure. For instance, the time signature 2/4 shows that there are 2 counts per measure and each count receives the time value of a quarter note. The time signature 4/4 indicates that there are four quarter notes per measure. The time signature 3/4 shows that there are three quarter notes per measure.

Since tablature cannot conveniently indicate a note value longer than a quarter note, we will use the quarter as a basis for longer notes. Just as notes are named after numerical fractions, they also add like fractions. The addition of two notes is indicated by a *tie*, a curved line joining the two notes whose time values are to be summed. This is illustrated in Figure J where two quarter notes are tied to form a note

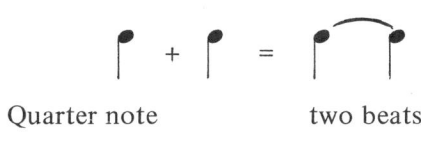

Quarter note   two beats

Figure J

that has a time value equal to two beats; it is thus called a half note. Similarly, we can, by addition of quarter notes, get notes of three beat or four beat duration as shown in Figure K.

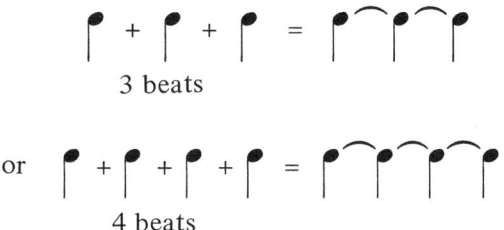

Figure K

Again, as in fractions, note values of less than one quarter are indicated by correspondingly smaller fractions. Thus, a note receiving only half the time value of a quarter note is called an eighth note. An eighth note is indicated by a *flag* attached to its stem as shown in Figure L. A note of time value one half that of an eighth note is called a sixteenth note and is indicated by two flags as shown in the second portion of Figure L.

Figure L

When eighth notes follow each other it is customary to join their flags into a *beam*. This does not combine the time values of the two eighth notes as does the tie; this is shown in Figure M.

Figure M

Silences or *rests* in music notation and tablature are indicated in the same way as notes. The quarter rest ( ) is the basis and is a silence of the same time value as a quarter note. Other rests correspond to the associated note time values: eighth rest ( ), a sixteenth rest ( ), a half rest ( ).

Most of the music in this volume uses only quarter notes, eight notes and quarter rests. This simplifies matters considerably.

When a portion of a song is to be played twice, it is enclosed within two sets of double bars with dots. These are called repeat marks and are illustrated in Figure N.

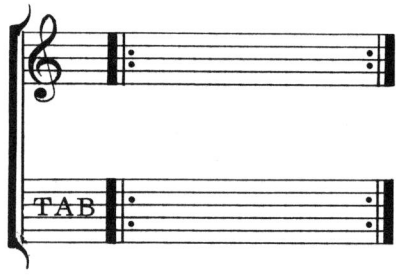

Figure N

The hammer is a note that is made to sound, **not** by the right hand, but by the *left hand.* One "hammers" the strings by bringing the fingers of the left hand down on the string hard enough to make the string sound as it strikes the **fret**. More sound can be obtained if the string is first sounded by the right hand in the normal fashion and then hammered by the left hand.

The hammer in the tablature is indicated by the letter "H" as shown in Figure O. It usually consists of two eighth notes which are connected by a curved line called a *slur line* (not to be confused with the tie. The tie connects two notes of the same pitch making a longer note but the slur line connects two notes of different pitch, both of which are sounded.) The hammer usually starts by plucking an open string. The left hand finger is then hammered down on the fingerboard of the guitar so that the second note of the pair is sounded.

To play the tablature given in Figure O, hold down the C chord as shown. Lift the second finger of the left hand so that the fourth string is open. With the thumb of the right hand sound the fourth string open as indicated in the tablature. Now replace the second finger into the normal C chord position. But instead of simply putting it down on the fourth string at the second fret, hammer it down so that the second note sounds. The rhythm of this figure is two eighth notes.

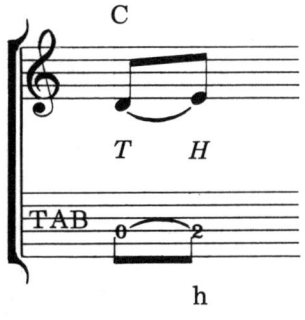

Figure O

The second form of embellishment is called by many names, the pick, pick-off, pull-off, but we'll simply call it the *picked note* and it will be symbolized in the tablature by the letter "P" as

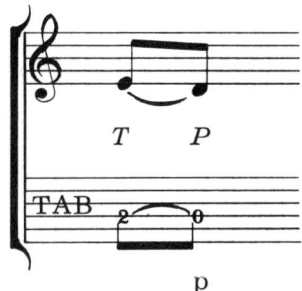

Figure P

shown in Figure P. The picked note is also sounded by the left hand but quite differently from the hammer. The picked note is *plucked* by a finger of the left hand. To play the figure in the tablature above, sound the fourth string of a normal C chord. Then, while the note is still sounding, remove the second finger of the left hand from the fingerboard of the guitar by pulling that second finger into your hand and in the process pluck the fourth string causing it to sound open. The picked note starts with a fretted string which is sounded by the right hand and is completed by an open string sounded by the left hand. The rhythm of the pick is the same as that of the hammer; i.e., two eighth notes.

THE BASIC GUITAR KEYS

In this chapter our task will be to train the left hand to play more chords. This enables us to play songs in several of the common guitar keys.

In guitar-playing the key of C traditionally consists of the three chords C, F, and G7. The key of G also consists of three chords: G, C, and D7. The first two songs of this chapter will introduce the key of G and act as a review of Carter-style picking.

OH, SUSANNA — KEY OF G

Let us take a closer look at the three chords of the key of G: the G, C, and D7 chords. The C chord used in the key of G is identical to that used in the key of C. Thus, there remains only two new chords to be learned. The G chord is a close relative of the G7 chord used in the key of C as shown here in Figures 1 thru 4:

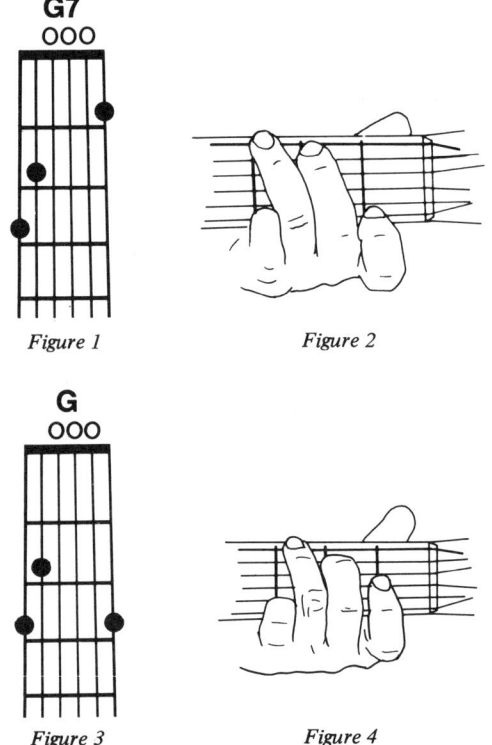

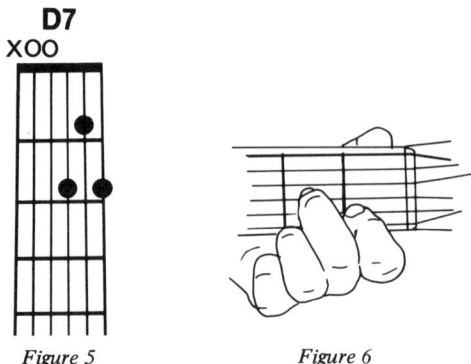

The D7 chord (Figures 5 and 6) should prove relatively easy. Recall that the "o" in the chord diagram (Fig. 5) means that the string is played open and the "x" indicates that the particular open string should not be sounded.

The most difficult measure in *Oh, Susanna* has been called out in the Chord Analysis Box. The first two beats of the 5th measure are played in the normal D7 position (Figures 7 and 8). The 3rd and 4th beats are played in a modified position (Figures 9 and 10) which leads quite easily and naturally into the G position (Figures 11 and 12).

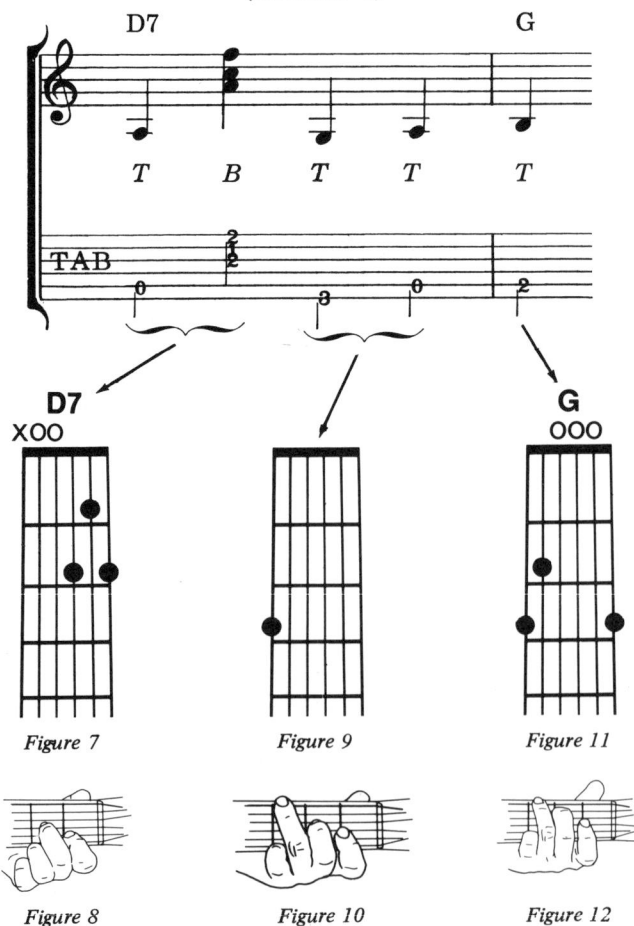

12

The letter "T" indicates that you play the corresponding note with the thumb. The letter "B" indicates that you brush the chord down with the index finger. When two B's appear together, brush down with the index finger on the first B and up with the index finger on the second.

Oh, Susanna-Solo

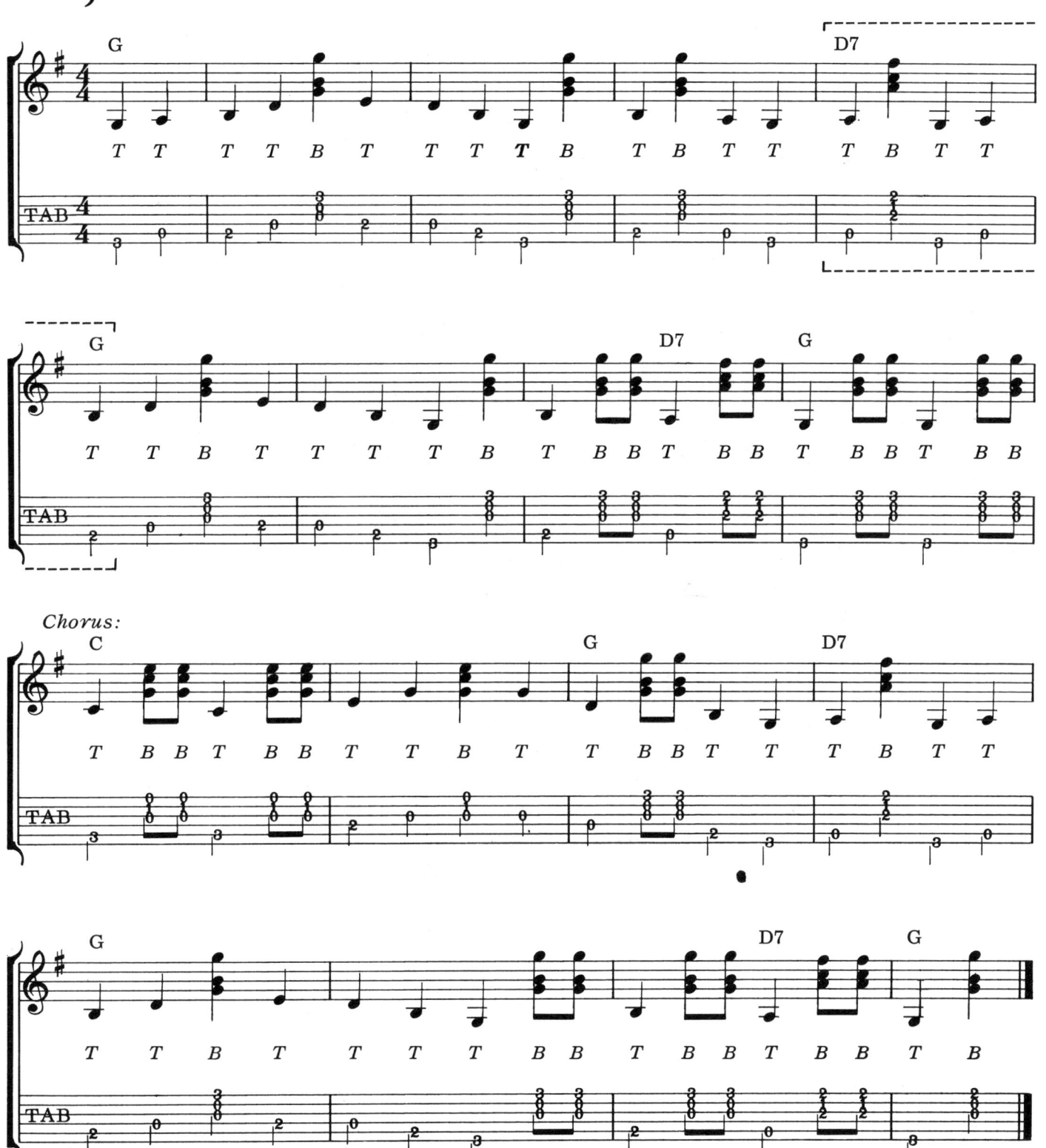

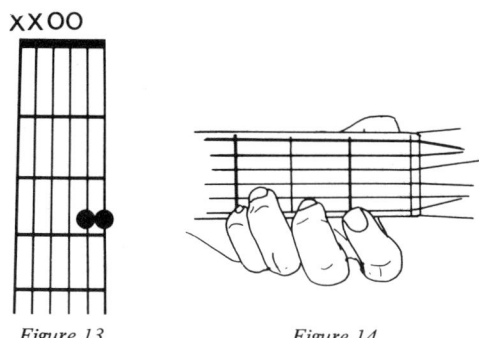

Figure 13   Figure 14

JESSE JAMES — CARTER-STYLE PICKING IN THE KEY OF G.

Two areas of difficulty are analyzed in this song. First, a modification of the G chord is needed in measure 6 (Figures 13 and 14) as is indicated in the music by an asterisk.

Second, the bass run from D7 to G in the 14th measure (See Chord Analysis Box) requires that the little finger fret the fourth string at the fourth fret. For many people this is quite difficult so a choice of chord positions is given. However, the position shown in Figures 17 and 18 is preferable to that in Figures 19 and 20.

CHORD ANALYSIS BOX — JESSE JAMES (measure 14)

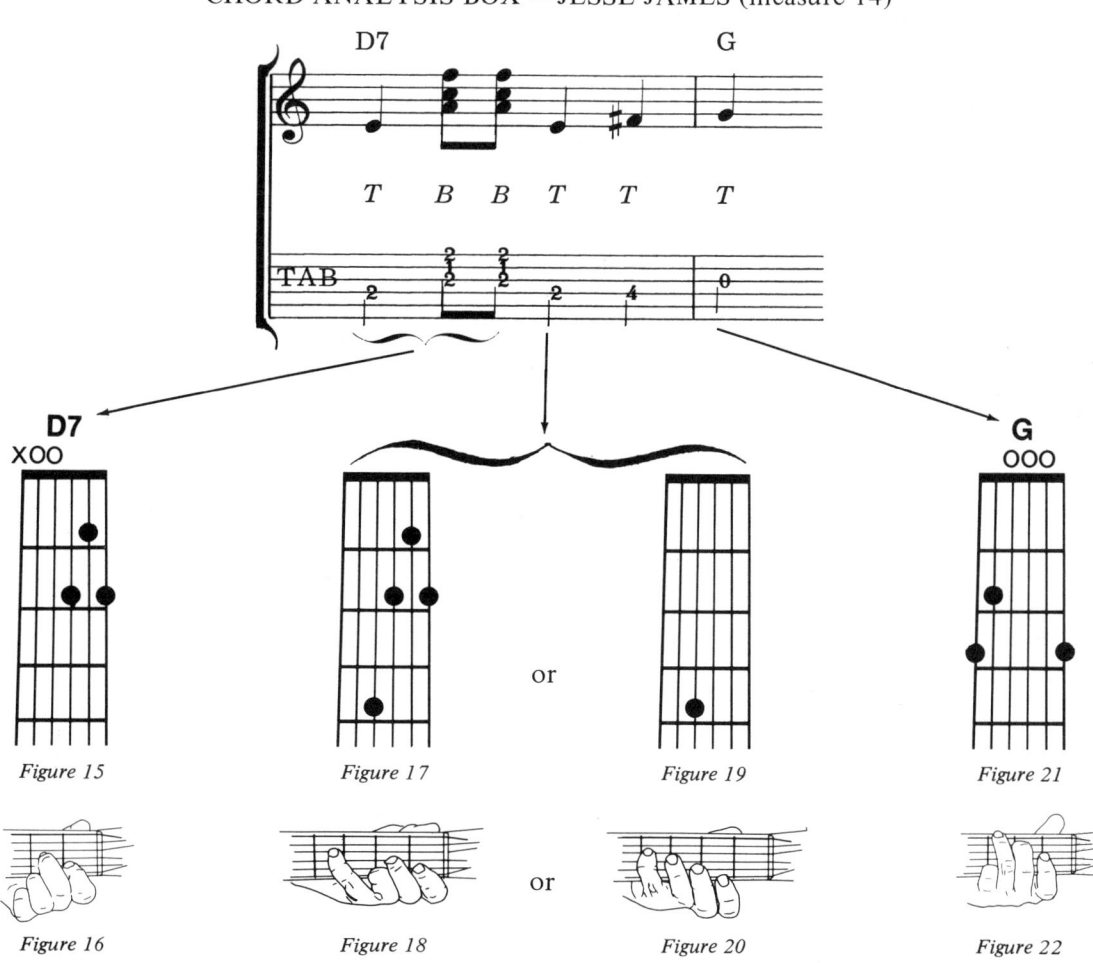

Figure 15   Figure 17   or   Figure 19   Figure 21

Figure 16   Figure 18   or   Figure 20   Figure 22

Jesse James - Solo

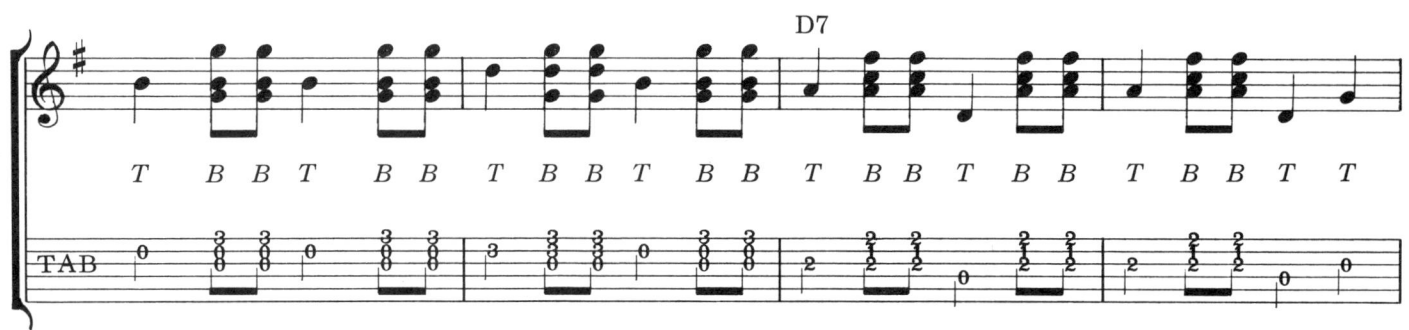

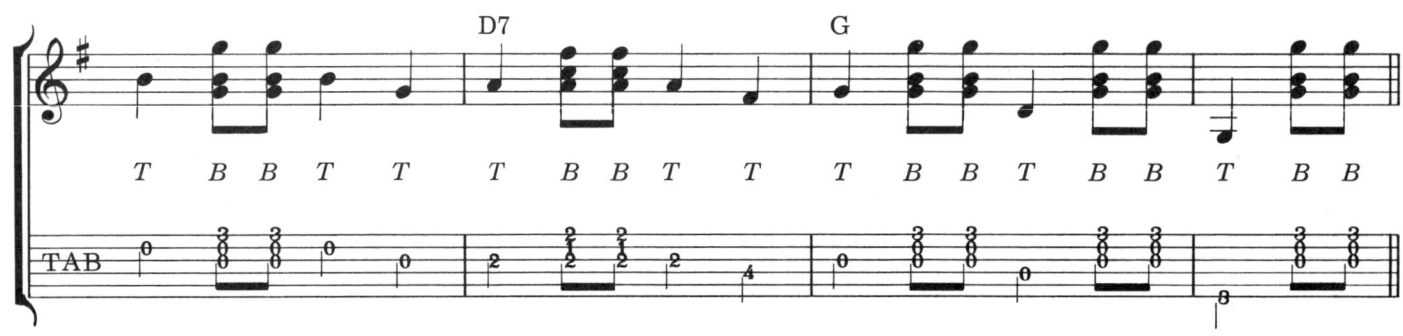

Chorus:

Jesse James - Melody

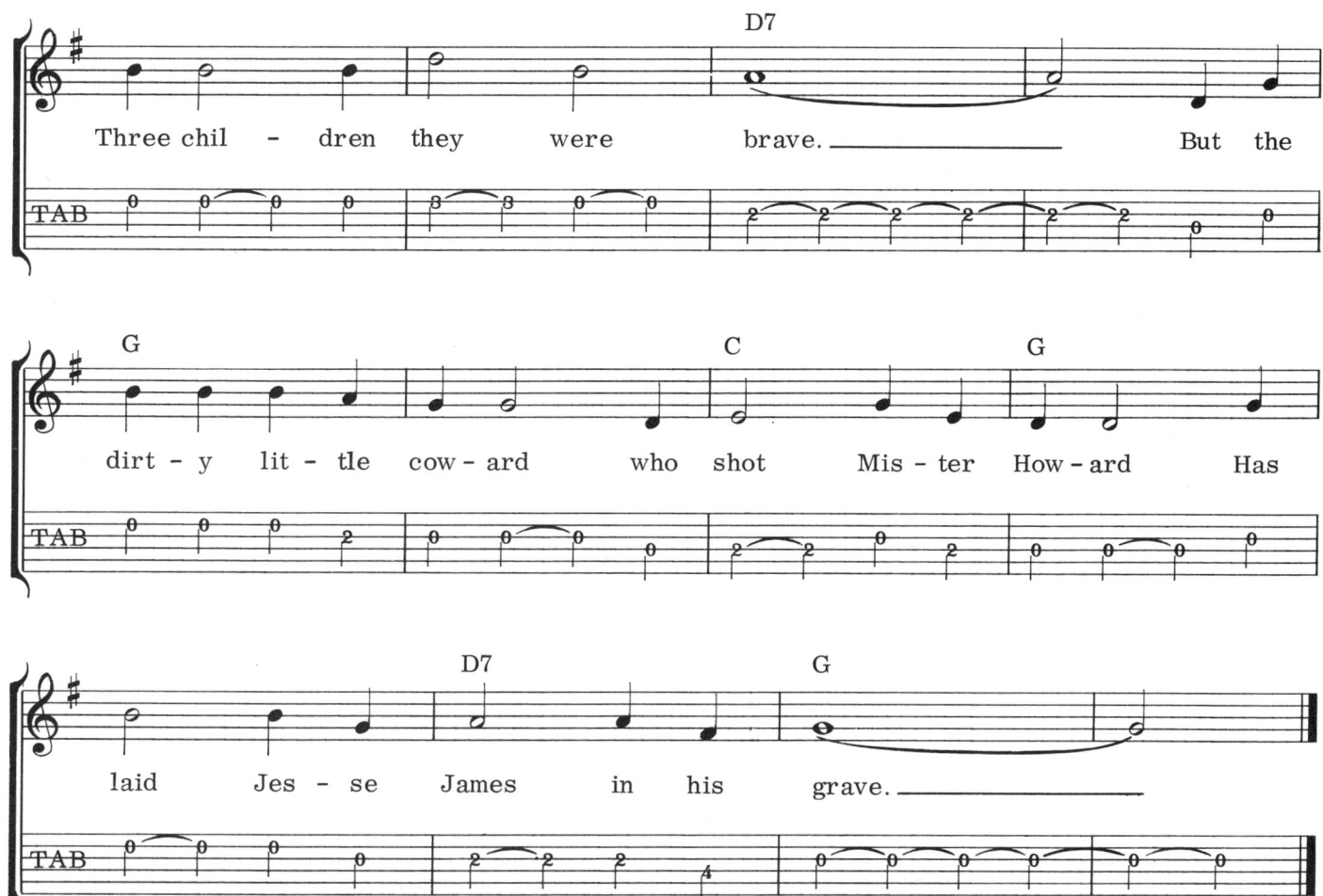

It was Robert Ford, that dirty little coward,
I wonder how he does feel,
For he ate of Jesse's bread and he slept in Jesse's bed,
And he laid poor Jesse in his grave.

It was on a Saturday night, Jesse was at home,
Talking with his family brave,
Robert Ford came along like a thief in the night
And laid poor Jesse in his grave.

This song was made by Billy Gashade,
As soon as the news did arrive;
He said there was no man with the law in his hand
Who could take Jesse James when alive.

LITTLE MAGGIE – THE D CHORD

This song introduces the D chord.

The little finger plays an important role in fingerpicking songs and it is necessary to achieve a certain amount of dexterity with it. *Little Maggie* should help you toward this goal.

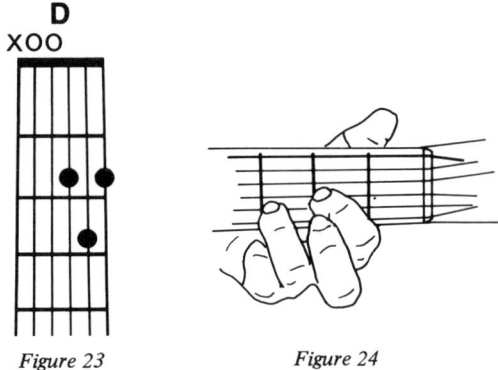

Figure 23   *Figure 24*

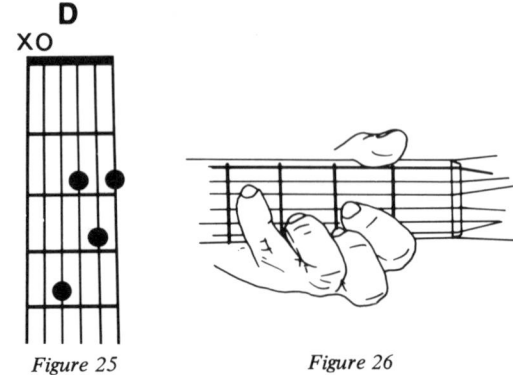

Figure 25   *Figure 26*

Little Maggie-Solo

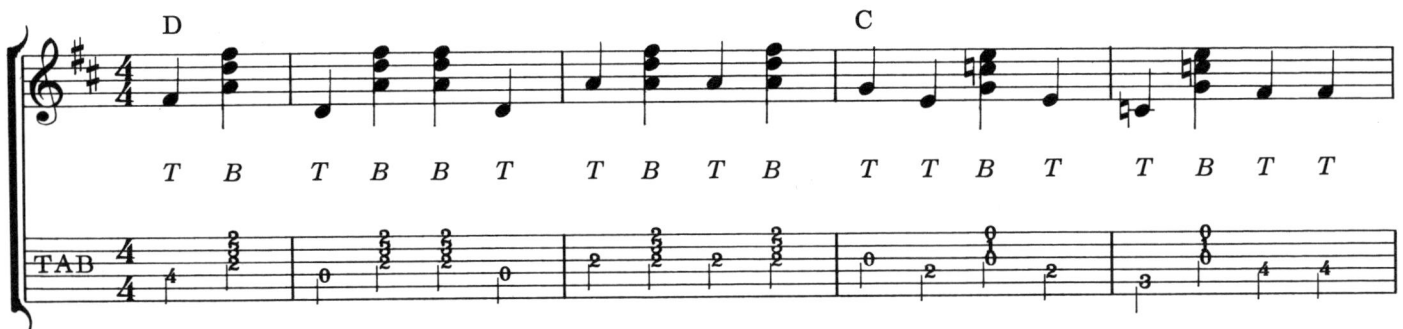

Little Maggie-Melody

Well, yonder stand little Maggie
With a dram glass in her hand;
She's drinkin' away her troubles
And foolin' with another man.

I'm goin' down to the station
With my suitcase in my hand;
I'm goin' to leave this country,
I'm goin' to some far distant land.

Oh, how could I ever stand it,
To see them two blue eyes,
Shining like the diamonds,
Like the diamonds in the sky.

The last time I saw little Maggie,
She was settin' on the banks of the sea,
With a fourty-four strapped around her,
And a banjo on her knee.

Sometimes I have a nickel
And sometimes I have a dime,
Sometimes I have five dollars
To pay little Maggie's fine.

I NEVER WILL MARRY — KEY OF D

This song introduces the key of D. The primary chords in this key are D, G, and A7. The A7 chord is illustrated in Figures 27 and 28.

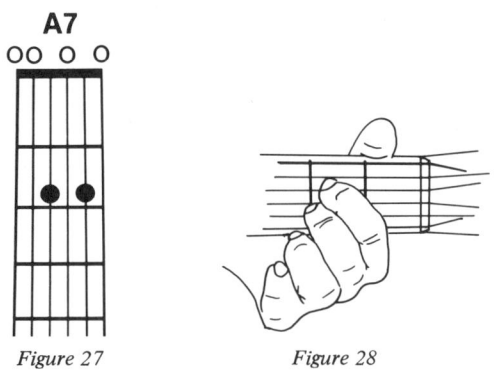

Figure 27 *Figure 28*

Measure 5 of the solo provides a challenge: the little finger is used to fret the fourth fret of the fourth string (Figures 31 and 32) and then is used in a pick-off (Figures 33 and 34).

CHORD ANALYSIS BOX — I NEVER WILL MARRY (measure 4)

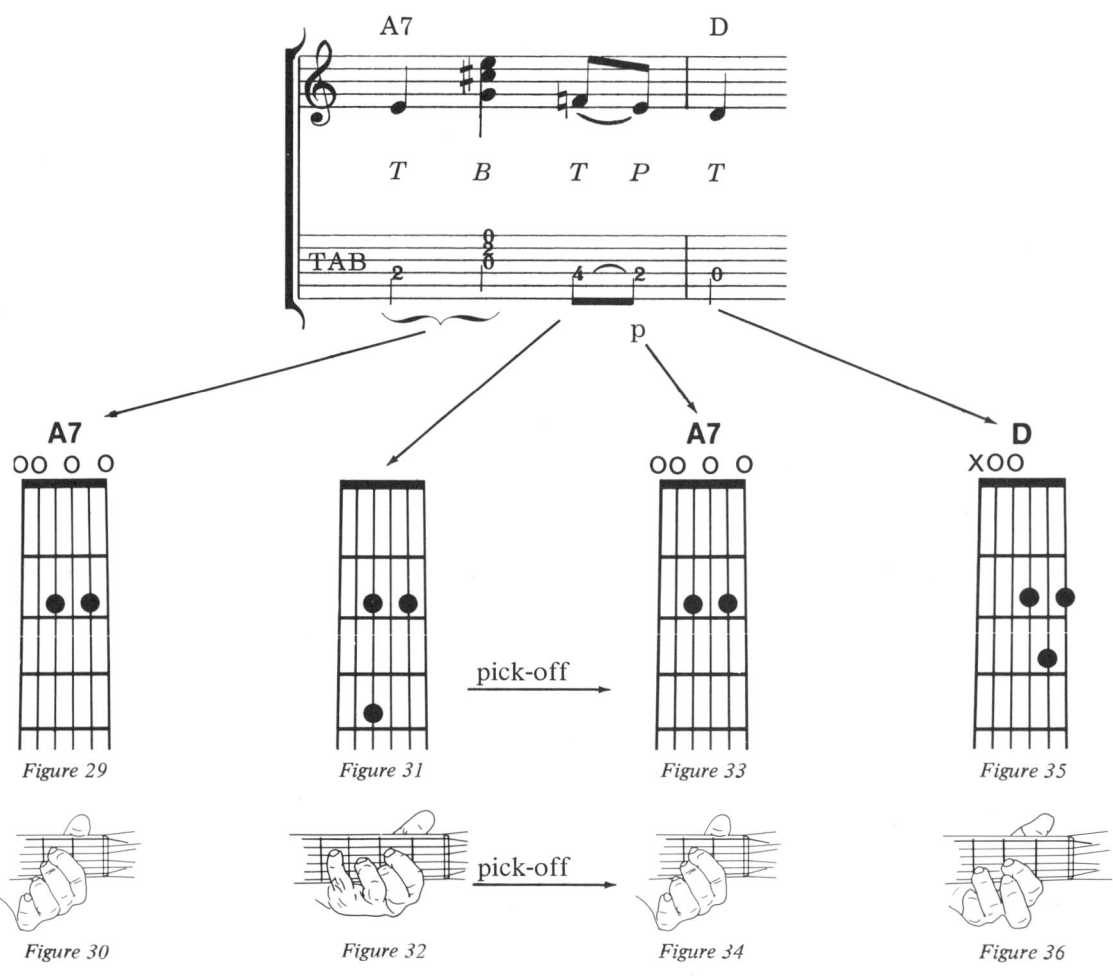

Figure 29 *Figure 31* *Figure 33* *Figure 35*

Figure 30 *Figure 32* *Figure 34* *Figure 36*

I Never Will Marry-Solo

I Never Will Marry-Melody

I heard a fair damsel
Making pitiful cry,
She sounded so lonesome
By the waters nearby.

"I never will marry,
"I'll be no man's wife,
"I intend to live single
"The rest of my life."

"The shells in the ocean
"Will be my death bed,
"The fish in deep waters
"Swim over my head."

She cast her fair body
In the waters so deep,
And she closed her pretty blue eyes
Forever to sleep.

RAILROAD BILL — THE E AND E7 CHORDS

Railroad Bill, a fingerpicking classic, introduces the E and E7 chords. These new chords can be fretted in two ways. The more common fingering of the E chord uses three fingers (Figures 37 and 38).

The second method of fretting the E chord uses only two fingers and is used extensively by experienced guitarists as it leaves two fingers free for fretting other notes (see Figures 39 and 40). This E chord position is slightly more difficult since the second finger must be used to fret two strings at the same time.

Since the two-finger E chord is more advanced, it should be learned as soon as possible, and it will be assumed that this position is used from now on.

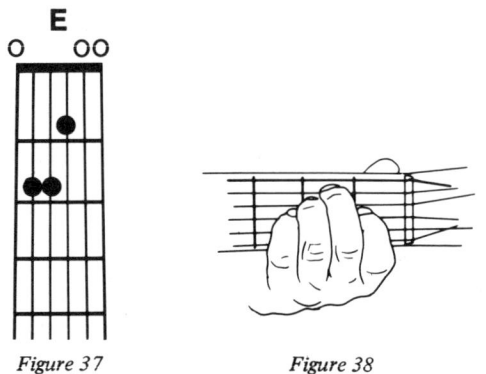

Figure 37   *Figure 38*

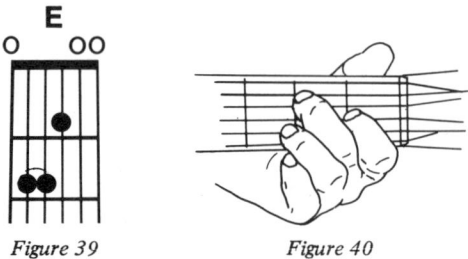

Figure 39   *Figure 40*

The E7 chord is a simple variation of either of the above E chords (Figures 41 and 42). It requires only the addition of the little finger at the third fret of the second string. The alternating bass for both the E and E7 chords uses the sixth string open and the fourth string at the second fret.

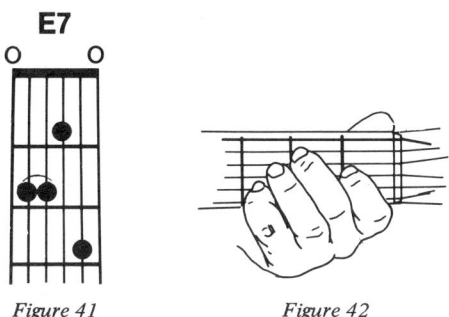

Figure 41   *Figure 42*

The most difficult portion of *Railroad Bill*, the transition between the E, E7 and F chords, has been detailed in the Chord Analysis Box shown below.

CHORD ANALYSIS BOX – RAILROAD BILL
(measure 6)

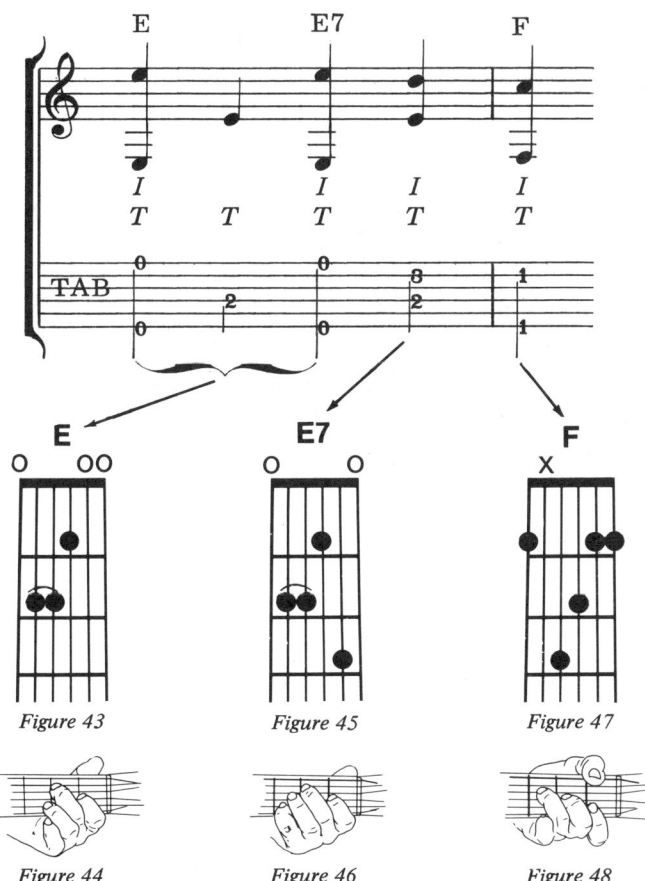

Figure 43   *Figure 45*   *Figure 47*

Figure 44   *Figure 46*   *Figure 48*

The letter "I" indicates that you play the corresponding note with the index finger of the right hand. The letter "M" indicates the middle finger.

25

Railroad Bill-Solo

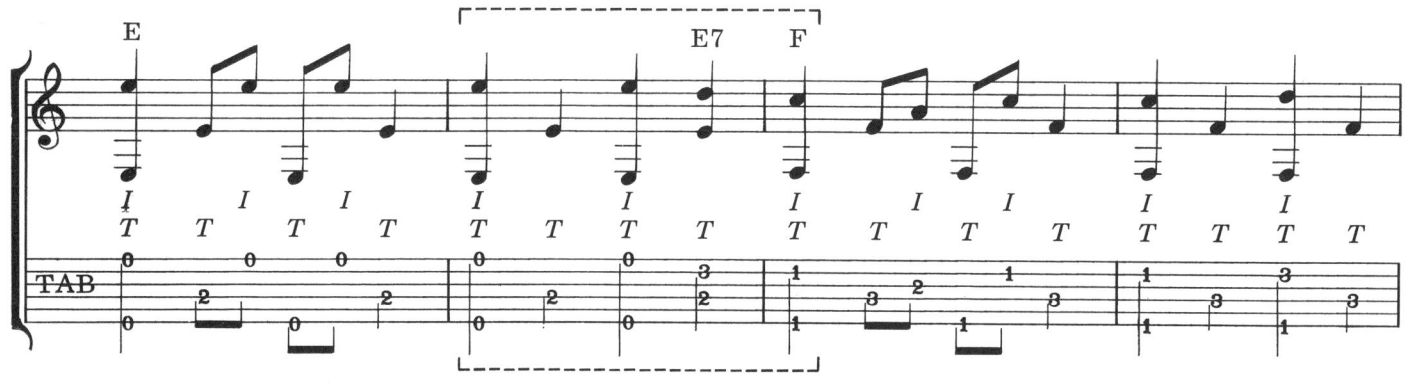
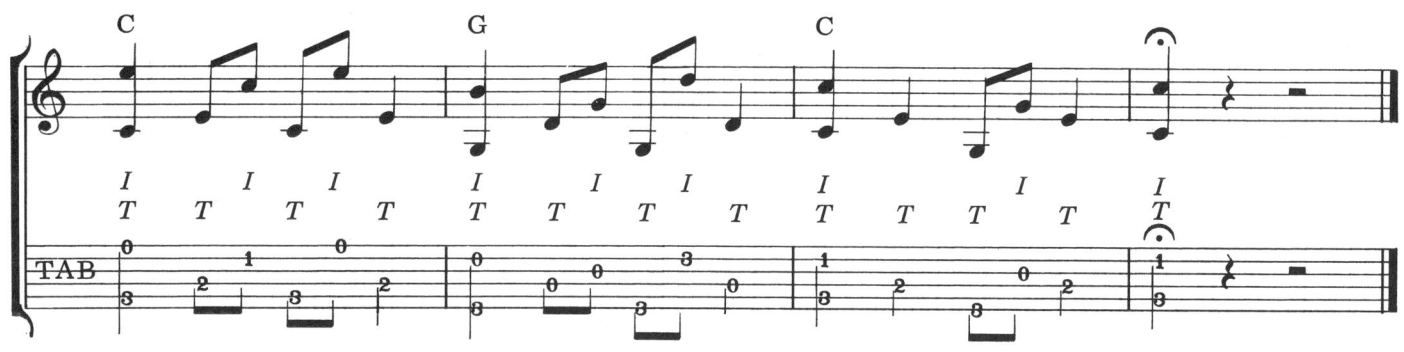
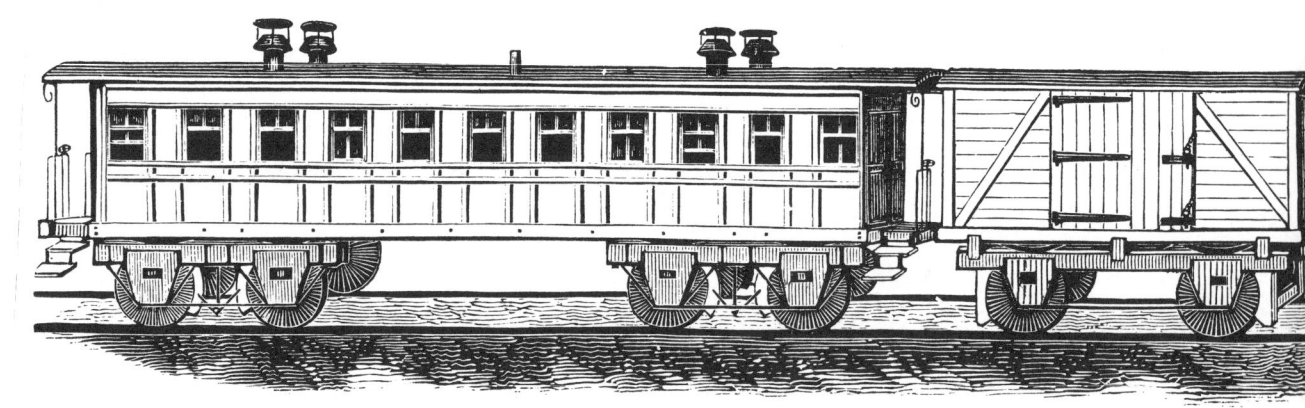

Railroad Bill-Melody

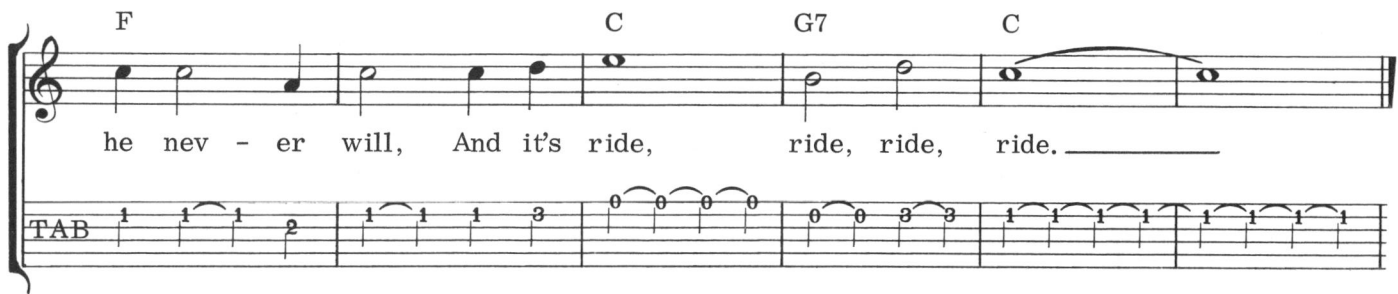

Railroad Bill was a mighty bad man,
Shot the light out o' the brakeman's hand,
And it's ride, ride, ride, ride.

Railroad Bill goin' over the hill,
Lightin' cigars with a ten-dollar bill,
And it's ride, ride, ride, ride.

Railroad Bill was a mighty big sport,
Shot the buttons off the sheriff's coat,
And it's ride, ride, ride, ride.

With a fourty-five special on a thirty-five frame,
How can I miss if I got dead aim?
And it's ride, ride, ride, ride.

Gonna get me a gun, gonna get me a charm,
Gonna kill anybody ever done me harm,
And it's ride, ride, ride, ride.

Kill me a chicken, send me the wing,
They think I'm workin', but I ain't doin' a thing,
But ride, ride, ride, ride.

JOHN HARDY – KEY OF A

We now introduce the key of A, which consists of the A, D, and E7 chords. Two of these chords have already been discussed; the D chord (Figures 23 and 24) and the E7 chord (Figures 41 and 42). The A chord is quite similar to the A7 chord (Figures 27 and 28).

As in the case of the E chord, there are two methods of playing the A chord. The first method uses three fingers to hold down the three strings of the chord (Figures 49 and 50). This leaves the little finger for fretting notes out of the chord.

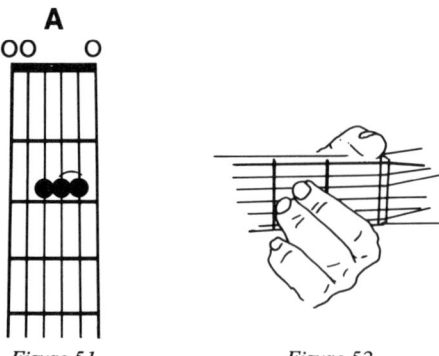
Figure 51   *Figure 52*

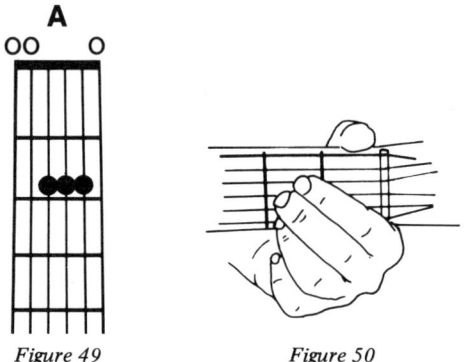
Figure 49   *Figure 50*

The second method (Figures 51 and 52) uses the middle finger to fret two strings at the same time. This method leaves both the third and fourth fingers free to play other notes and is used widely by traditional and advanced guitarists.

The beginner should use that method of fretting the A chord which gives the best results. However, the technique of fretting two strings with one finger is quite important and should be learned as soon as possible. In the following discussion of the music, it will be assumed that the "two-finger" form of the A chord is being used.

The solo version of *John Hardy* uses some "out-of-the-chord" notes which at first may appear difficult. In the 3rd measure, the first string is fretted at the third fret with the little finger while the D chord position is held. The second string open in the 4th measure is best achieved by lifting the whole A chord on the third beat and replacing it for the fourth beat.

John Hardy-Solo

John Hardy-Melody

RED RIVER VALLEY — MORE KEY OF A

Before attempting to play the solo version of *Red River Valley*, make sure you can play the melody notes easily. Work for the little finger has been outlined in the Chord Analysis Box. Notice that in Figures 63 through 66, the bass notes used in the alternating bass have been changed to include the sixth string. Normally the principal and alternate bass strings for an A chord would be the fifth and fourth strings.

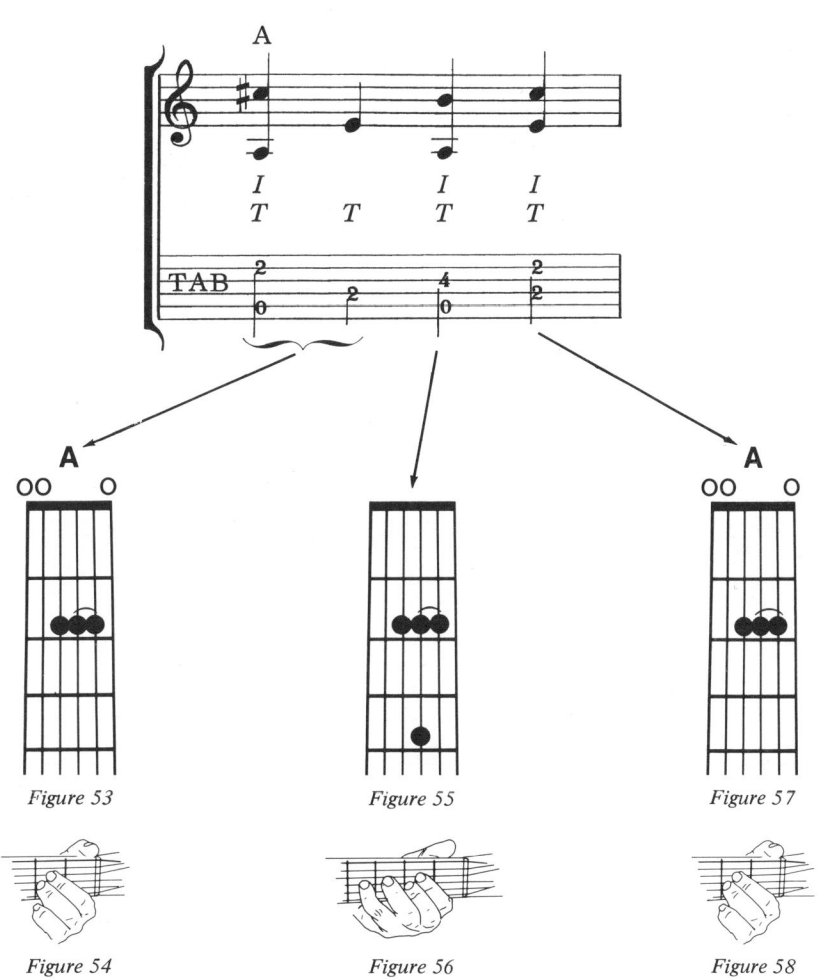

CHORD ANALYSIS BOX — RED RIVER VALLEY (measure 2)

Figure 53

Figure 54

Figure 55

Figure 56

Figure 57

Figure 58

CHORD ANALYSIS BOX — RED RIVER VALLEY (measures 12-13)

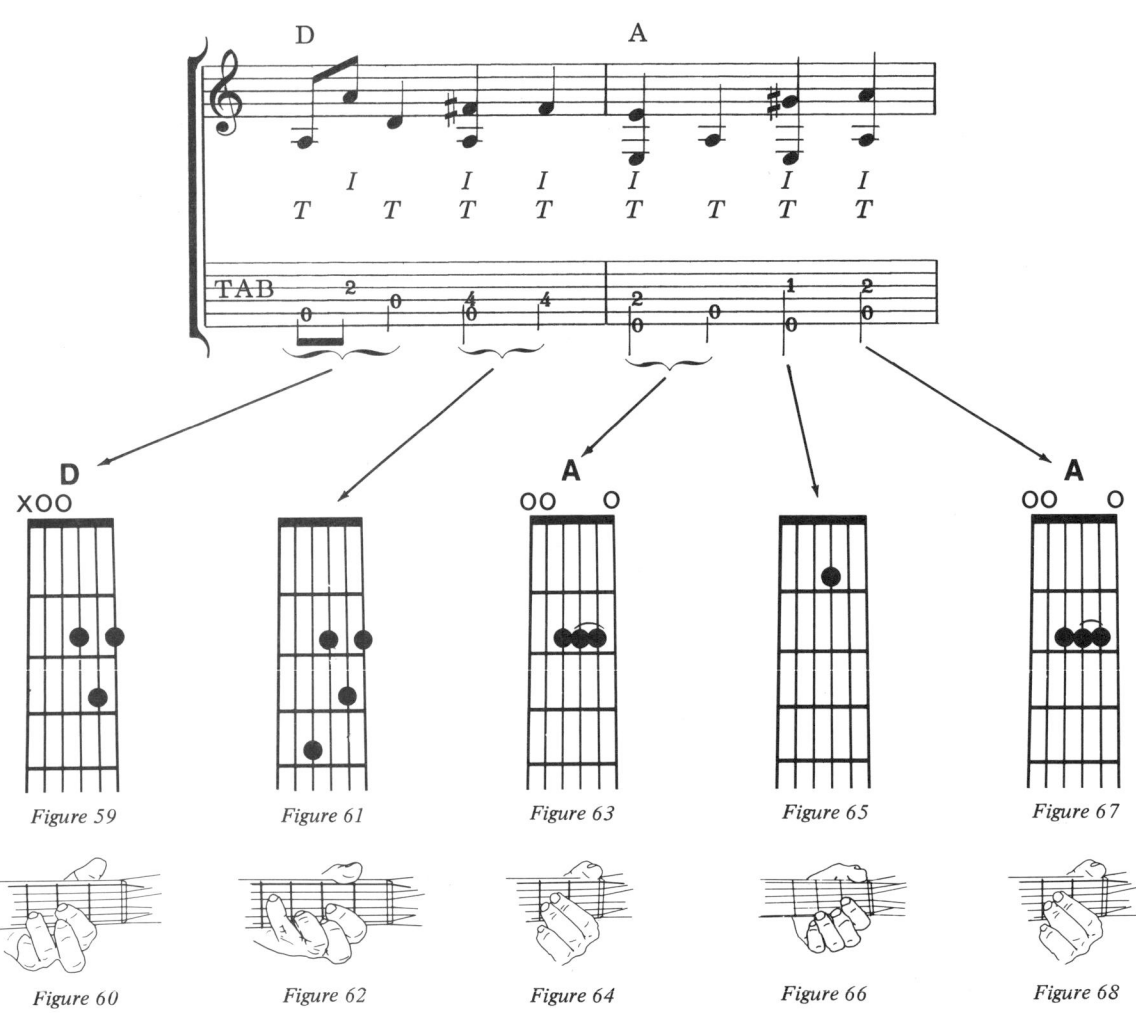

Figure 59   Figure 61   Figure 63   Figure 65   Figure 67

Figure 60   Figure 62   Figure 64   Figure 66   Figure 68

Red River Valley-Solo

Red River Valley - Melody

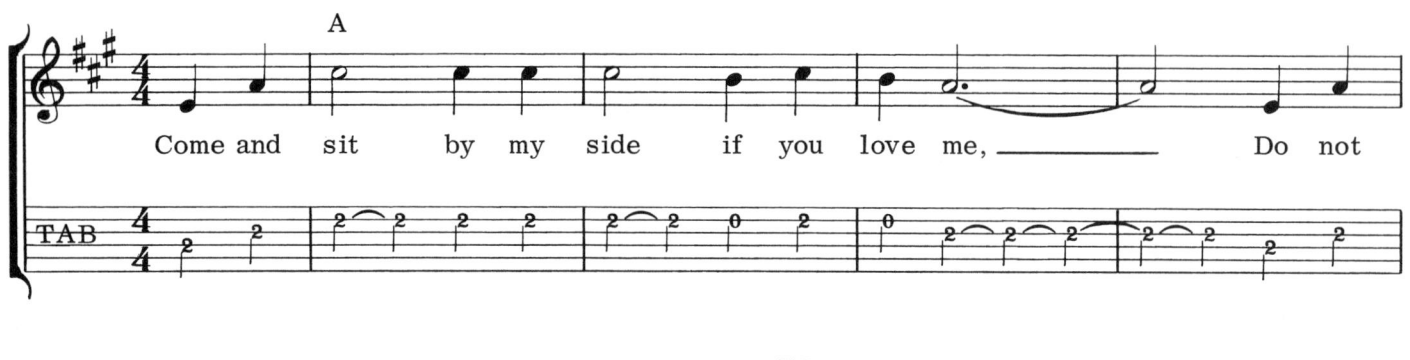

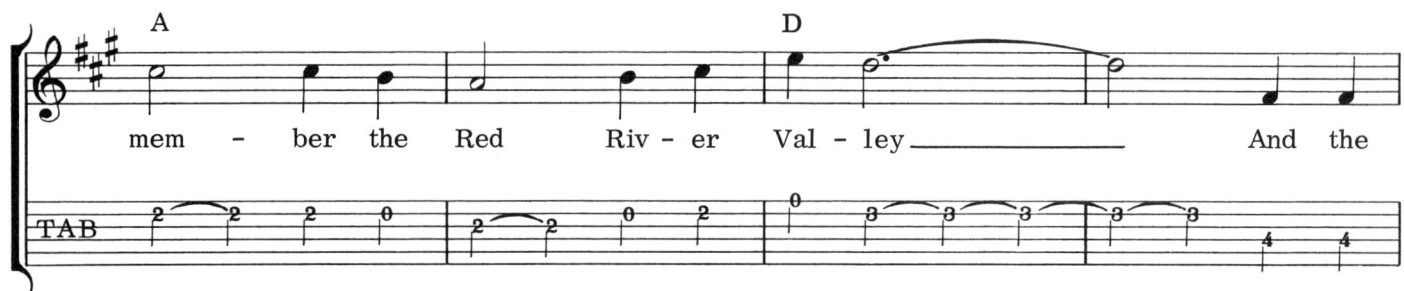
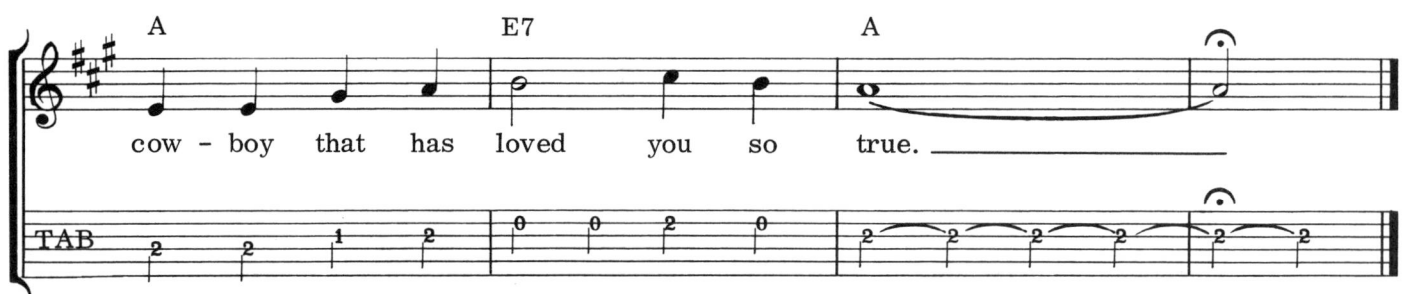

Won't you think of this valley you're leaving,
Oh, how lonely, how sad it will be,
Oh, think of the fond heart you're breaking,
And the grief you are causing to me?

From this valley they say you are going,
We will miss your bright eyes and sweet smile,
For they say you are taking the sunshine
Which has brightened our pathways a while.

As you go to your home by the ocean,
May you never forget those sweet hours,
That we spent in the Red River Valley,
And the love we exchanged 'mid the flowers.

LITTLE ROSEWOOD CASKET – THE LONG A CHORD

We will use a new form of the A chord in this song—often called the "long A." This chord requires a *barre* (pronounced "bar") which simply means that one finger is used to fret several strings at once on the same fret. We have already done this in the F, A, and E chords where one finger was used to fret two strings. In the long A, however, the index finger must fret four strings at once. First try the partial chord using only the index finger (Figures 69 and 70). Notice that the "flat" of the index finger is used to fret the strings. In this practice position the second, third, and fourth strings must be properly fretted. Once these three strings sound clean, add the little finger at the first string, fifth fret (Figures 71 and 72). The use of the "long A" is shown in the Chord Analysis Box below. Try this one measure several times before trying the whole song. It is quite typical of the use of the long A chord.

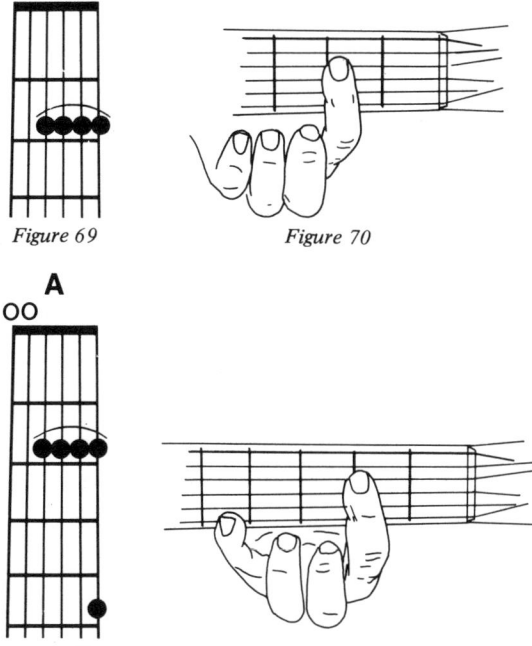

Figure 69 *Figure 70*

Figure 71 *Figure 72*

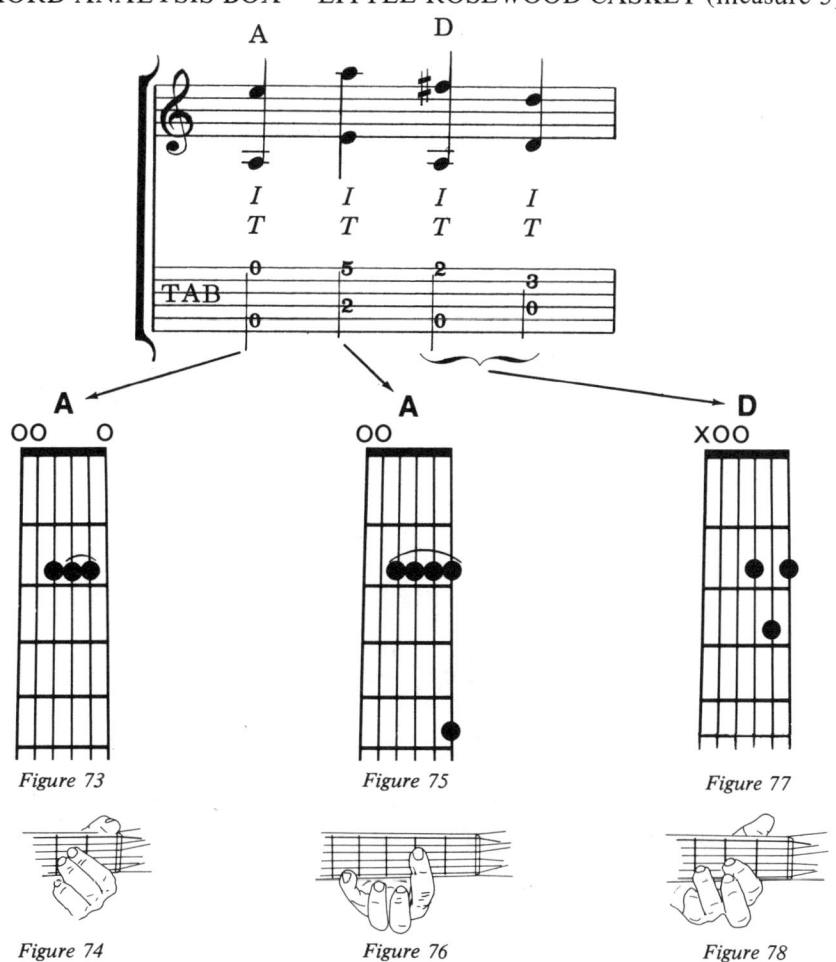

CHORD ANALYSIS BOX – LITTLE ROSEWOOD CASKET (measure 5)

Figure 73 *Figure 75* *Figure 77*

Figure 74 *Figure 76* *Figure 78*

35

Little Rosewood Casket-Solo

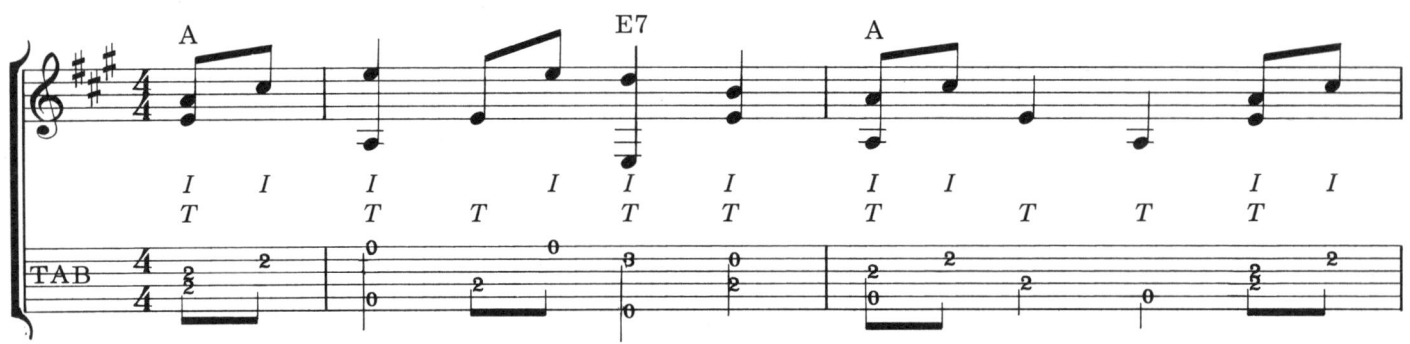
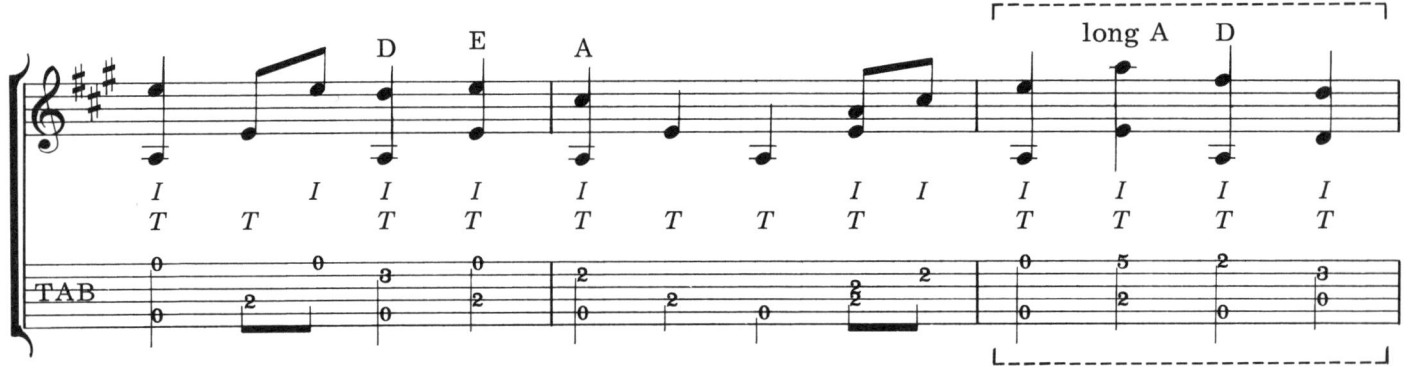
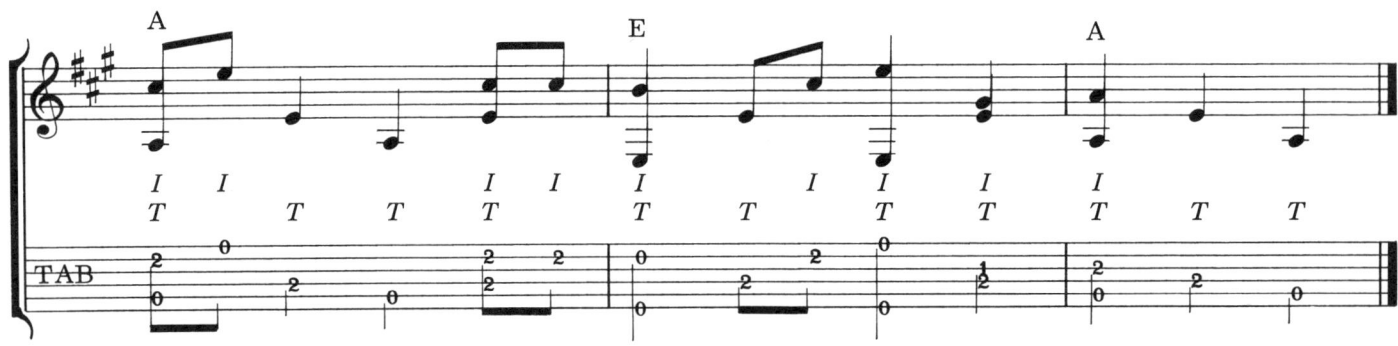

Little Rosewood Casket-Melody

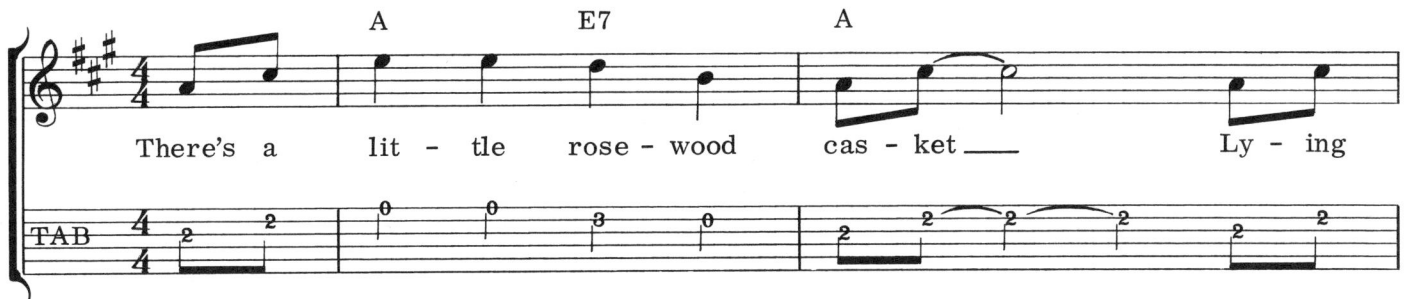

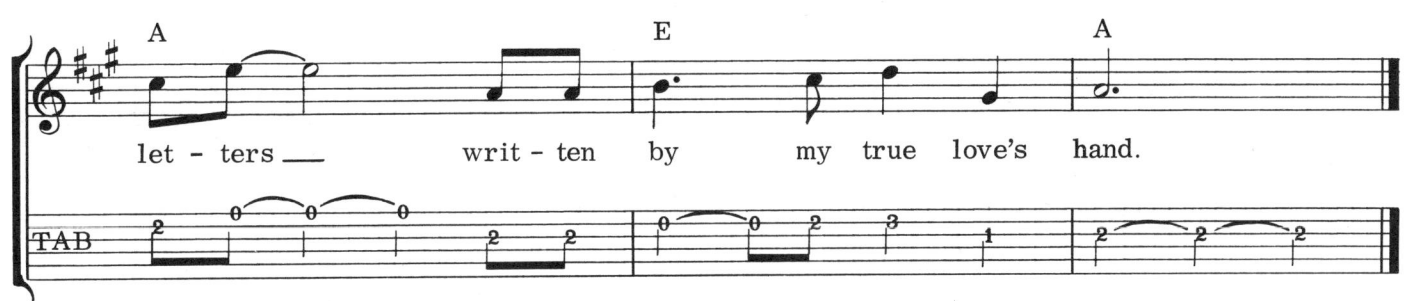

Come and sit beside me, brother,
Come and sit upon my bed,
Come and lay your head upon my pillow,
For my aching heart falls dead.

Last Sunday I saw him walking,
With a lady by his side,
And I thought I heard him tell her
She could never be his bride.

When I'm dead and in my coffin,
And my shroud's around me bound,
And my narrow grave is ready
In some lonesome churchyard ground.

Take his letter and his locket,
Placed together o'er my heart,
But the golden ring he gave me
From my finger never part.

BANKS OF THE OHIO – LONG A IN THE KEY OF D

The long A can also be used to substitute for an A7 chord in the key of D as in this version of *Banks of the Ohio*. It is used quite simply in the 7th measure and should cause no difficulty.

An interesting chord used in this song is the A7 chord which is intermediate in hand positions between the regular A chord and the long A. As with many of the chords we have learned in this chapter, this A7 chord has two alternate fingering positions. The first uses the normal A chord (Figures 51 and 52) as the basis for the A7 position (Figures 79 and 80). As illustrated in the Chord Analysis Box, this chord position is often used for an A7 chord which follows the regular A chord.

The second finger position for the A7 chord is shown in Figures 87 and 88. As you will recognize, the barre of the long A chord is used but the first string is fretted at the third fret rather than at the fifth fret. This A7 chord is often used following the long A chord.

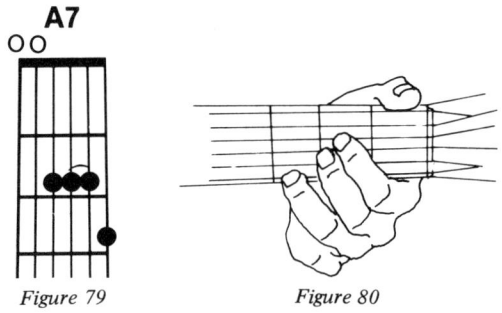

Figure 79   Figure 80

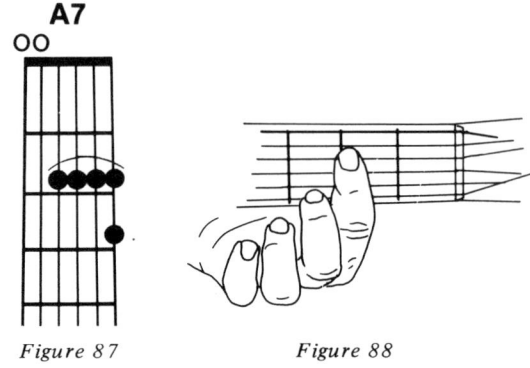

Figure 87   Figure 88

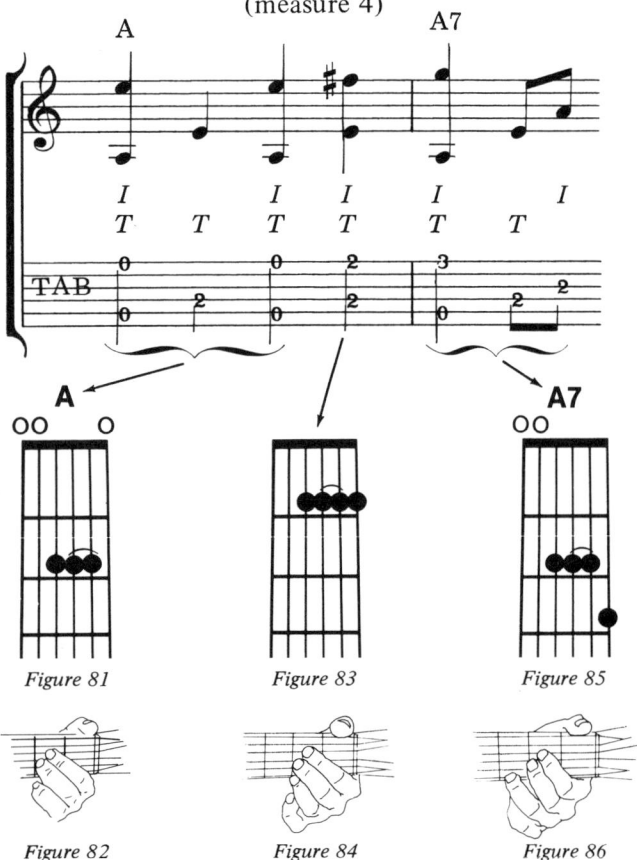

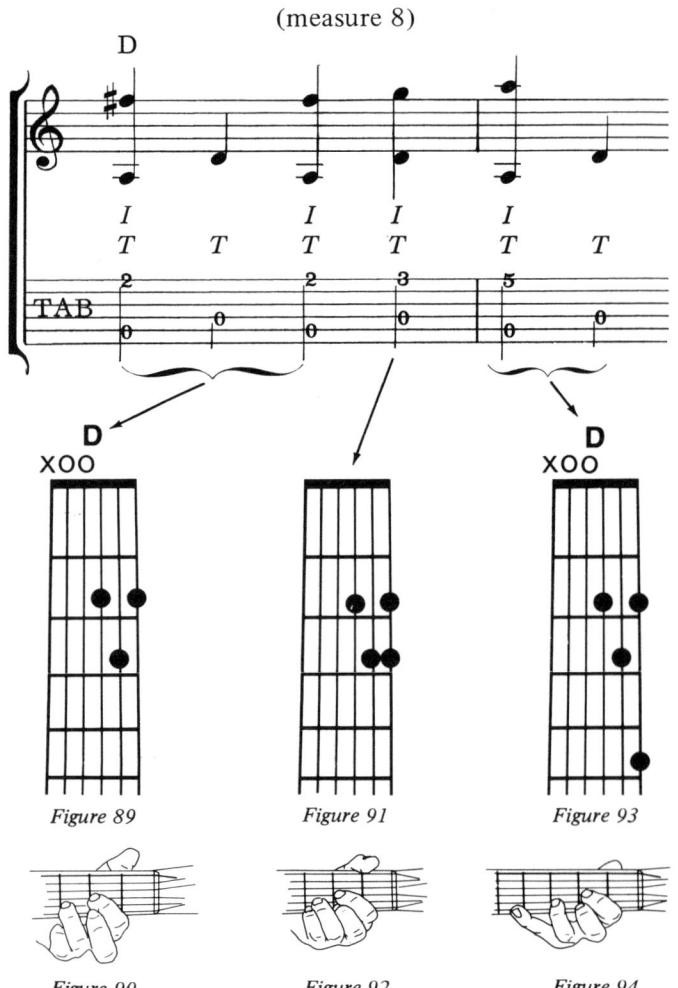

Banks of the Ohio - Solo

Banks of the Ohio – Melody

SUGAR BABE – KEY OF E

This song introduces the key of E which uses the chords E, A, and B7. The only unfamiliar chord is B7 (Figures 95 and 96). Notice that the middle finger is used to fret both the fifth and sixth strings at the second fret. The bass usually alternates from the sixth to the fourth string, but occasionally the fifth string may be substituted for either.

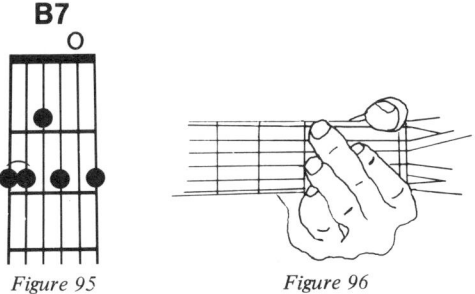

Figure 95   Figure 96

Sugar Babe-Solo

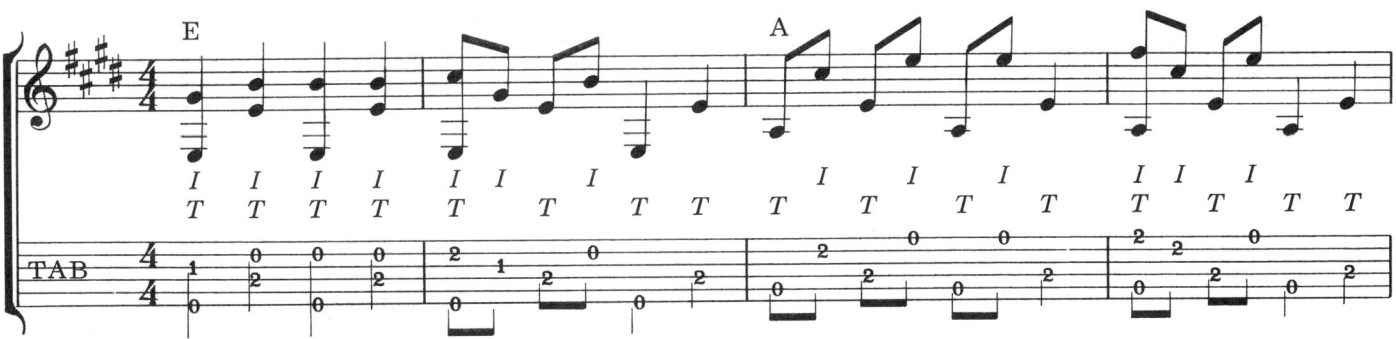

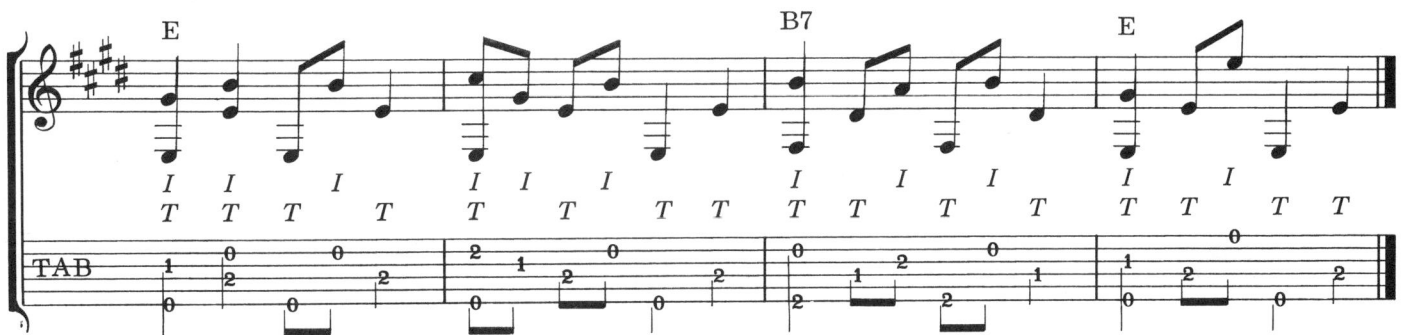

SUMMARY

In this chapter we learned how to play chords and a few solos in all the common keys used in folk guitar. You must learn which chords correspond to the various keys. As an aid, I suggest you study the table of keys and chords given:

Key	Chords
A	A, D, and E7
C	C, F, and G7
D	D, G, and A7
G	G, C, and D7
E	E, A, and B7

MORE CHORDS

Most of the songs we have learned use only the primary chords such as C, F, and G in the key of C. In the following songs, we will be learning several new chords to add to these three in various combinations.

THE GREAT SILKIE (CHILD #113)

This song is in the key of D and uses the chords D, G, and C. Notice the chord similarities in *Little Maggie* from the previous chapter. The fingering position in the 2nd measure is the same one used in *Little Maggie,* Figures 25 and 26. Play the melody alone a few times before trying the solo.

The Great Silkie-Solo

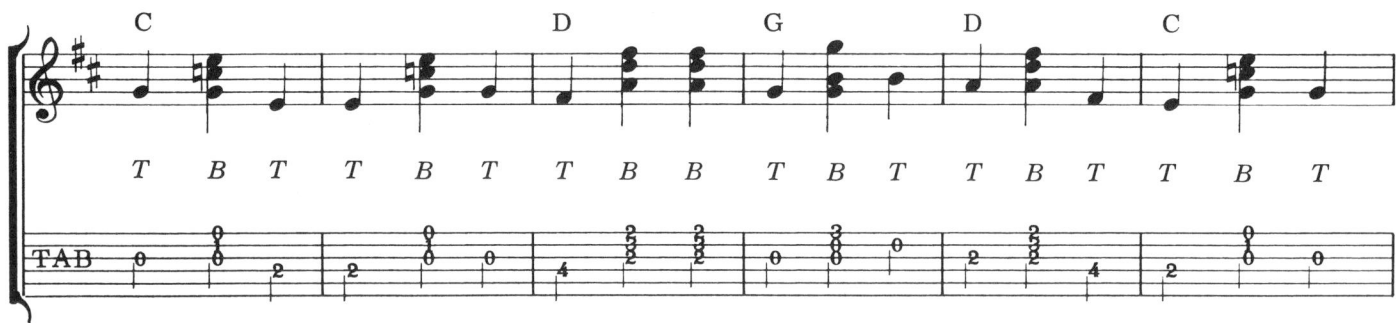

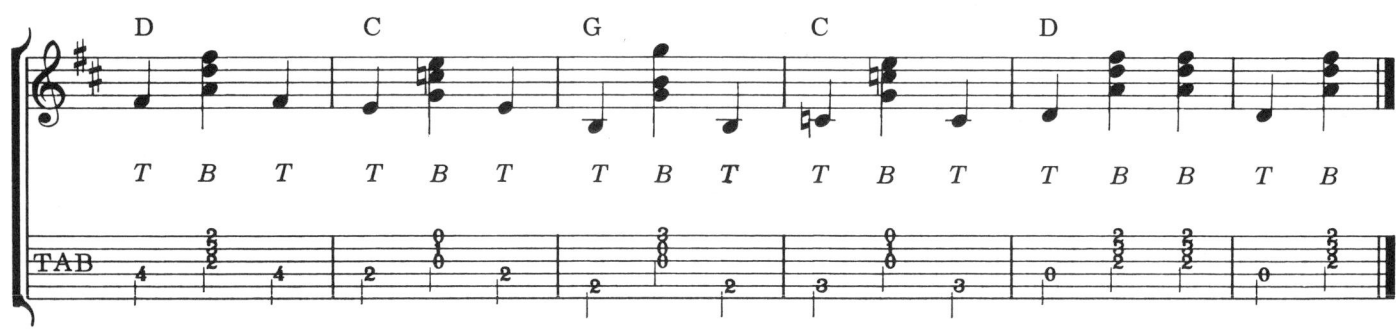

The Great Silkie-Melody

Then in steps he to her bed fit
And a grumlie guest I'm sure was he,
Saying, "Here am I, thy bairnis' father
"Although that I be not comelie."

"I am a man upon the land
"And I am a silkie in the sea,
"And when I'm far and far from land
"My home it is in Sule Skerry."

"It was na well," quo the maiden fair,
"It was na well, indeed," quo she,
"That the great silkie of Sule Skerry
"Should hae come and aught a bairn ta me."

Then he has taen a purse of gold,
And he has pat it upon her knee,
Saying, "Gie to me my little young son,
"And take thee up thy nourice fee."

"It shall come to pass on a simmer's day
"When the sun shines het on every stone
"That I shall take my little young son
"And teach him for to swim the foam."

"And thou shall marry a proud gunner
"And a proud gunner I'm sure he'll be,
"And the very first shot that ever he'll shoot
"He'll kill both my young son and me."

"Alas, alas," the maiden cried,
"This weary fate's been laid for me."
And then she said, and then she said,
"I'll bury me in Sule Skerry."

ACRES OF CLAMS — THE Am CHORD

The Am (A minor) chord, shown in Figures 97 and 98, is our first minor chord. Notice the similarity between the finger positions of the Am chord and the C chord; also notice the similarity between the A and the Am chords.

The fingering of the Am chord is easy to learn when you notice that it is identical to that of the E chord (Figures 37 and 38) *but* moved toward the first string. The principle bass of the Am chord is the fifth string open, the alternate bass notes are the fourth string at the second fret or the sixth string open. These are the same as the A and A7 chords.

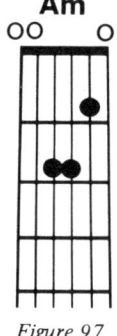

Figure 97

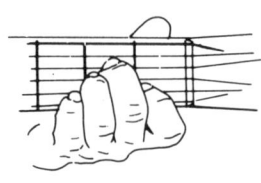

Figure 98

Acres of Clams-Solo

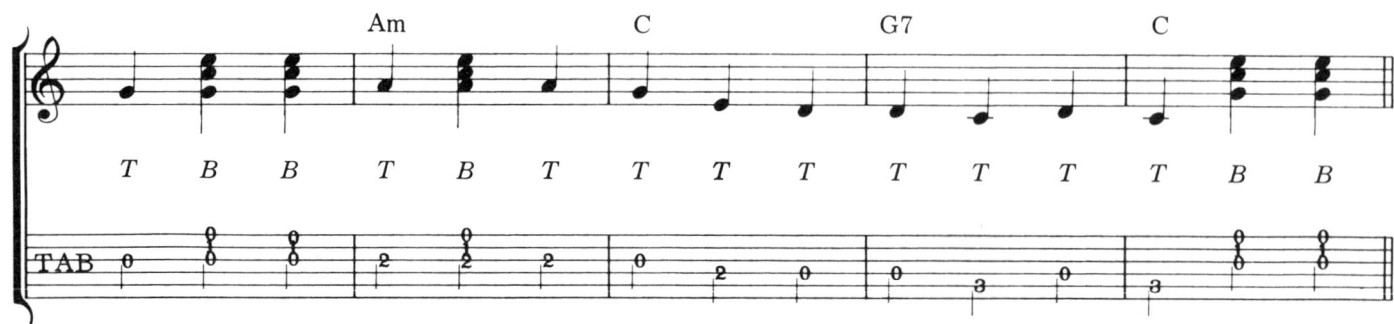

Refrain:

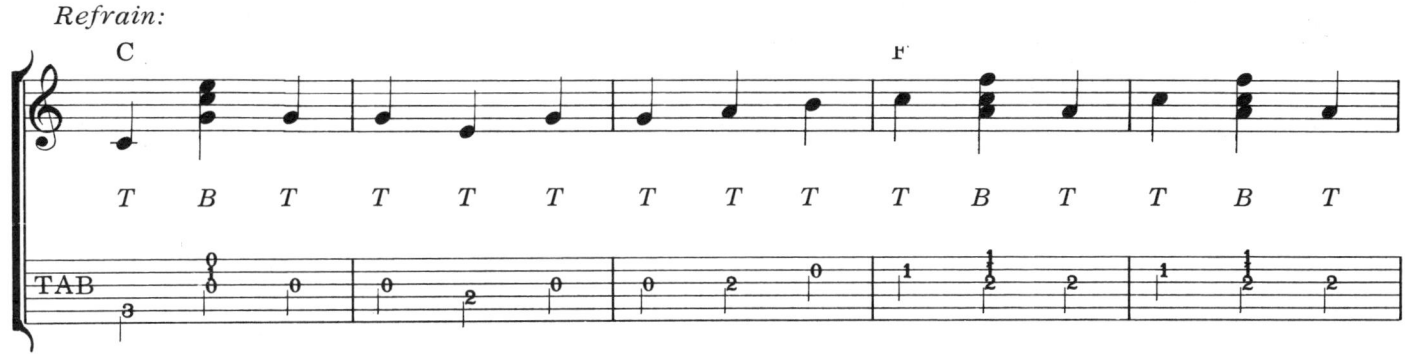

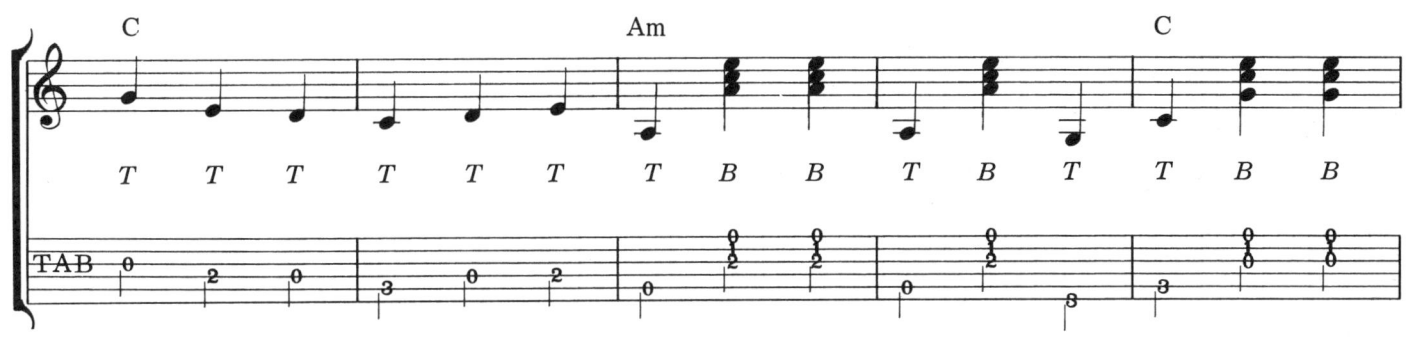

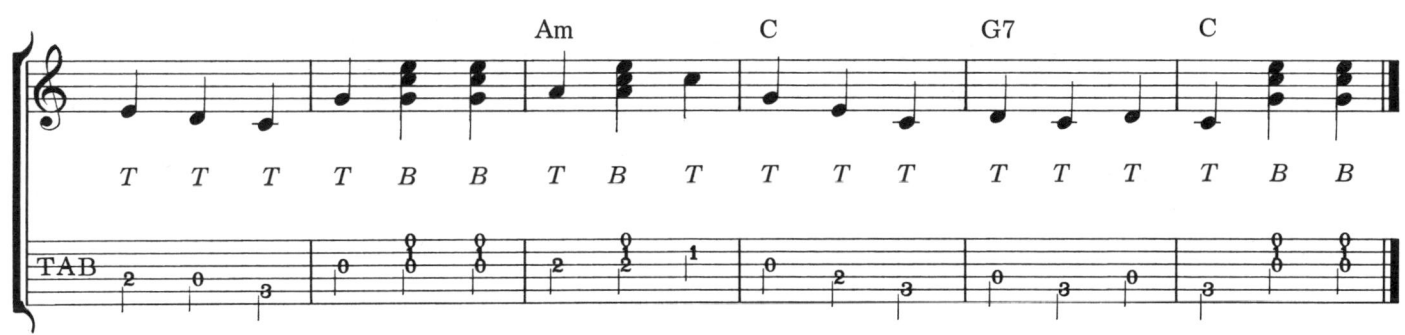

Acres of Clams - Melody

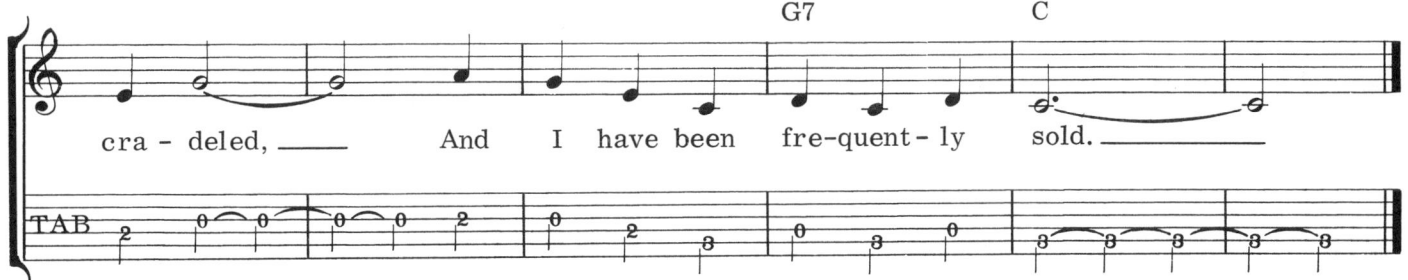

cra - deled,____ And I have been fre-quent-ly sold.____

For one who gets riches by mining,
Perceiving that hundreds grow poor,
I made up my mind to try farming
The only pursuit that is sure.
The only pursuit that is sure, etc.

So rolling my grub in a blanket,
I left all my tools on the ground,
And started one morning to shank it
For a country they call Puget Sound.

I tried to get out of the country,
But poverty forced me to stay
Until I became an old settler
Now you couldn't drive me away.

No longer the slave of ambition
I laugh at the world and its shams.
I think of my happy condition
Surrounded by acres of clams.

COLUMBUS STOCKADE BLUES — MORE Am CHORDS

This song uses slightly more complex Carter-style picking than did *Acres of Clams*. For instance, notice that in the 15th measure the hammer must be done with the little finger. *Columbus Stockade Blues* will take some practice but the effort is worthwhile.

Columbus Stockade Blues-Solo

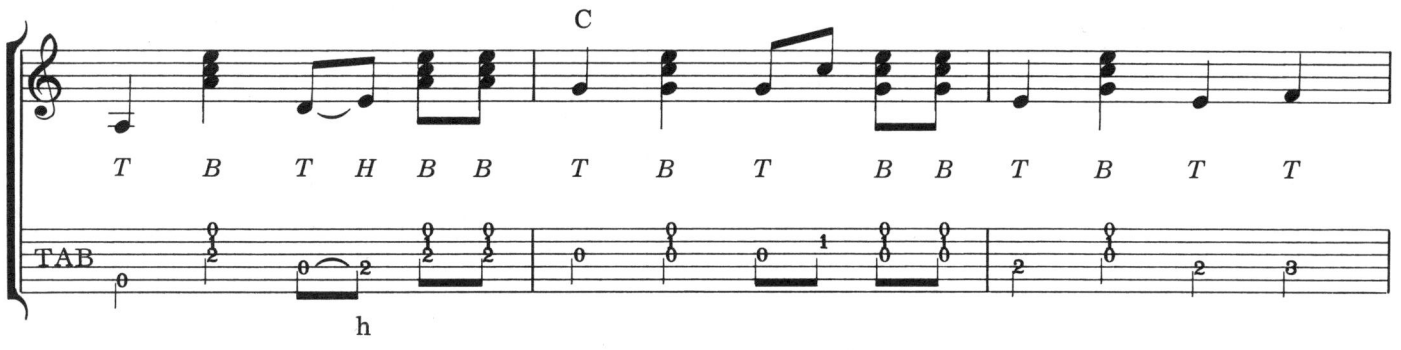
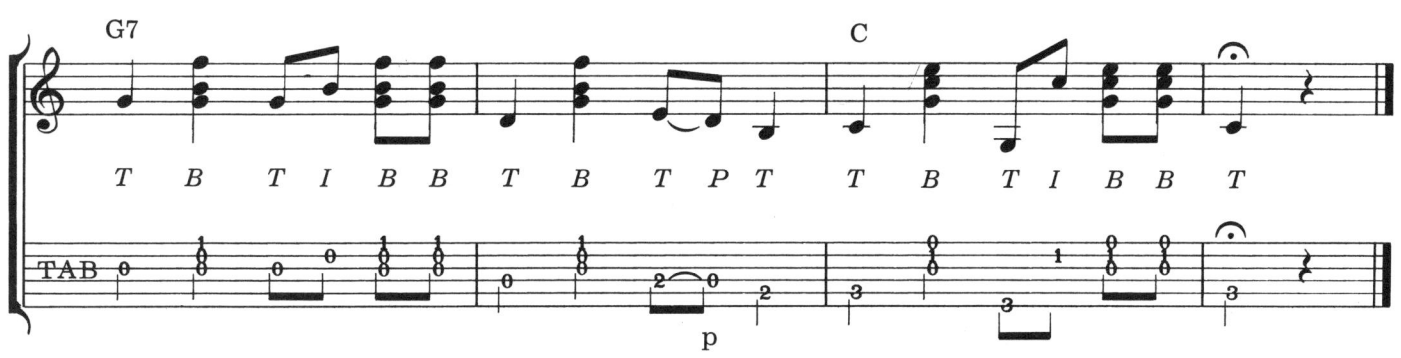

Columbus Stockade Blues-Melody

Last night as I lay sleeping,
I dreamed I held you in my arms,
When I woke, I was mistaken,
I was peering through those prison bars.

HOUSE OF THE RISING SUN

This song combines many of the chords we have learned in this and previous chapters. It is in the key of C and uses the C, F, G, Am, D, and E7 chords.

House of the Rising Sun-Solo

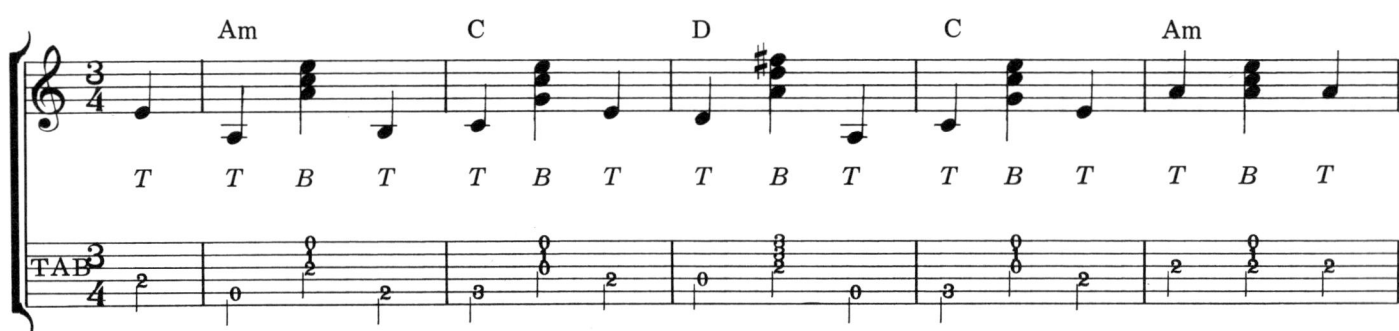

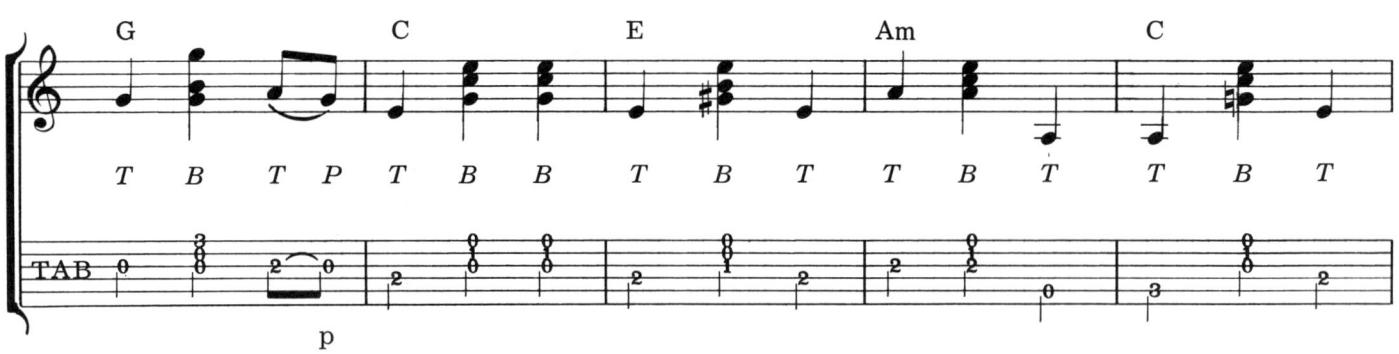

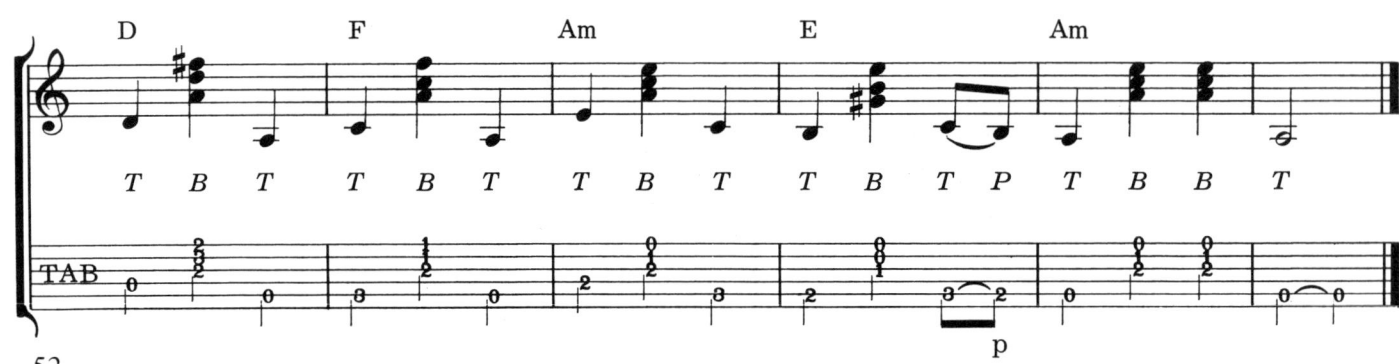

House of the Rising Sun-Melody

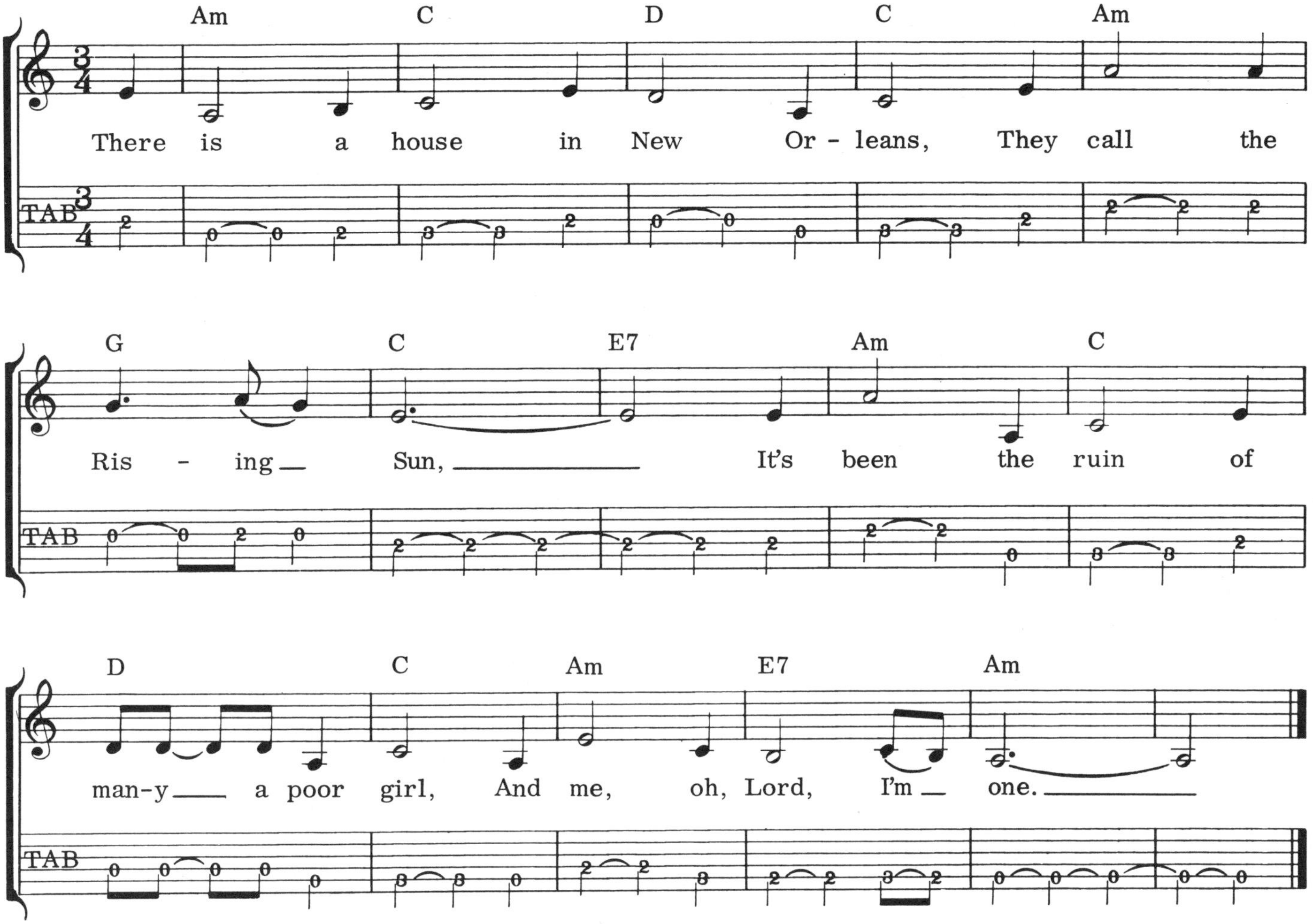
Am C D C Am
There is a house in New Or - leans, They call the
TAB
G C E7 Am C
Ris - ing Sun, It's been the ruin of
TAB
D C Am E7 Am
man-y a poor girl, And me, oh, Lord, I'm one.
TAB

Go tell my baby sister
Never to do like I done,
Beware of that house in New Orleans
They call the Rising Sun.

I'm going back to New Orleans,
My race is almost run.
I'm going back to spend my life
Beneath the Rising Sun.

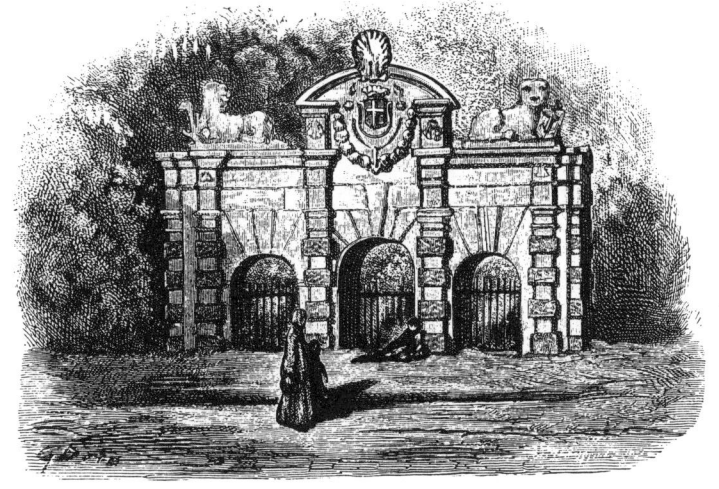

CRUEL WAR IS RAGING—FINGERPICKING Am CHORDS

The Am chord is often combined with the C chord as in *Cruel War Is Raging*. Since both chords use the same strings for the alternating bass, you will get an interesting sound when playing both chords using the same right hand figures.

The thumb must be used carefully when the fingers are picking consecutive eighth notes (see Chord Analysis Box). If you are unsure of how to do this, review *Sugar Babe* at the end of the previous chapter.

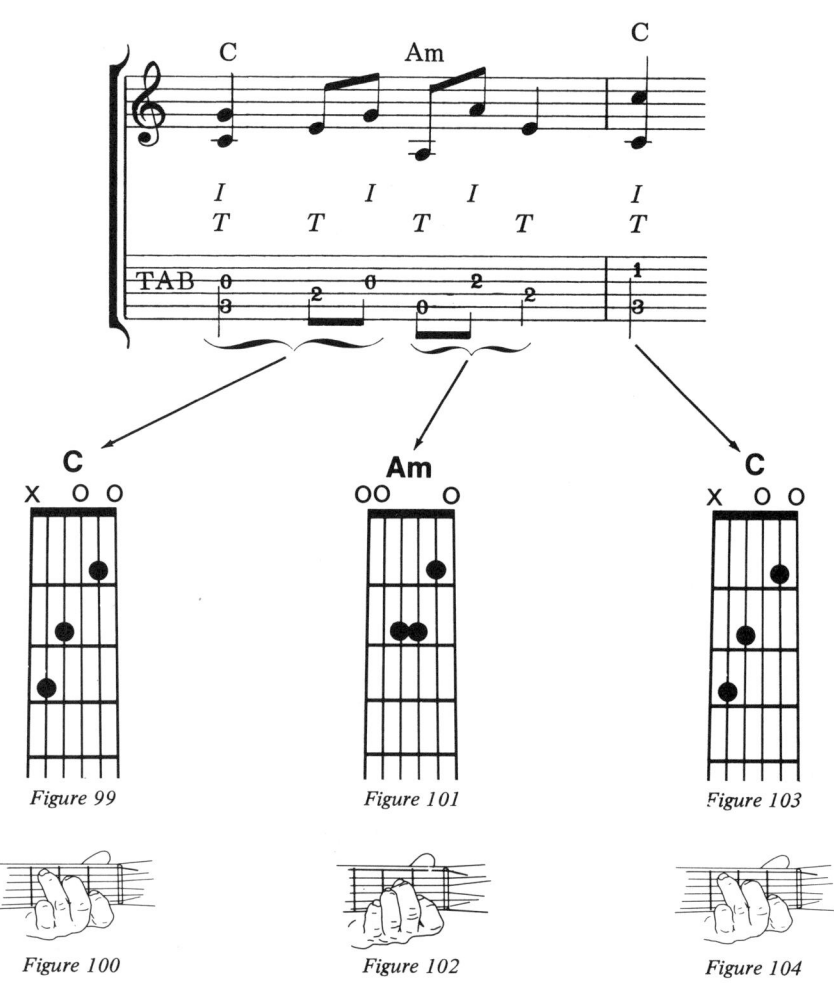

Figure 99

Figure 100

Figure 101

Figure 102

Figure 103

Figure 104

CHORD ANALYSIS BOX — CRUEL WAR IS RAGING (measure 11)

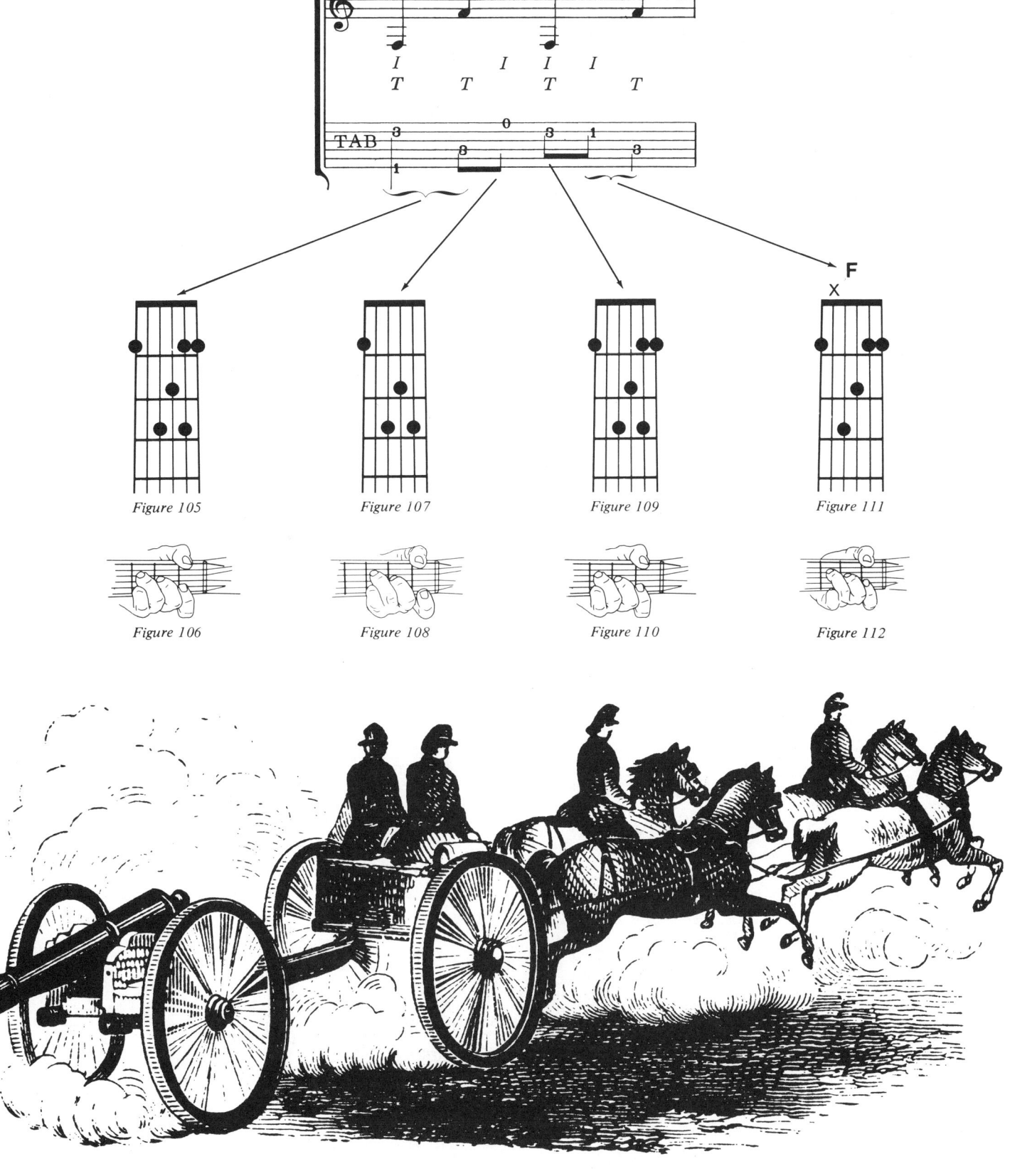

Figure 105

Figure 107

Figure 109

Figure 111

Figure 106

Figure 108

Figure 110

Figure 112

Cruel War is Raging-Solo

Cruel War is Raging-Melody

57

Tomorrow is Sunday and Monday is the day
That your captain calls for you and you must obey.
Your captain calls for you; it grieves my heart so.
Oh, let me go with you. No, my love, no.

I'll go to your captain, go down upon my knees,
Ten-thousand gold guineas I would give for your release,
Ten-thousand gold guineas; it grieves my heart so.
Oh, let me go with you. No, my love, no.

Your waist it is too slender, your fingers are too small,
Your face it is too tender to face the cannon's ball.
Your face it is too tender; it grieves my heart so.
Oh, let me go with you. No, my love, no.

Oh, Johnny; Oh, Johnny; I think you are unkind,
I love you far better than all of mankind.
I lover you far better than tongue can express.
Will you let me go with you? Yes, my love, yes.

I'll roach back my hair, men's clothes I'll put on,
I'll pass as your comrade as we march along;
I'll pass as your comrade, none will ever guess.
Won't you let me go with you? Yes, my love, yes.

SCARBOROUGH FAIR (CHILD #2) — THE Dm CHORD

We will add one more minor chord to our repertoire: the Dm chord. This chord is illustrated in Figures 113 and 114 shown below. The Dm is the relative minor of F. The bass notes for the fingerpicking alternating bass are the same as the D and D7 chords.

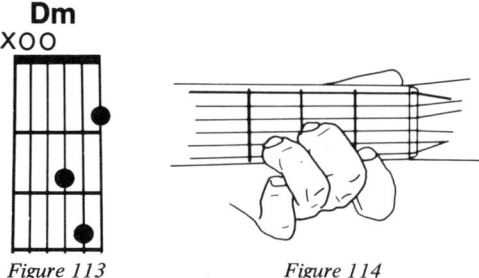

Figure 113 *Figure 114*

Scarborough Fair-Solo

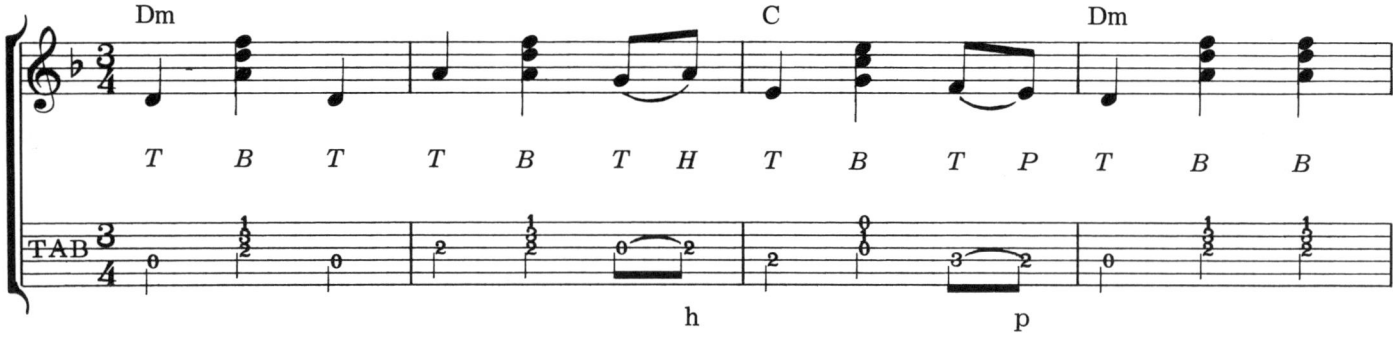

Scarborough Fair-Melody

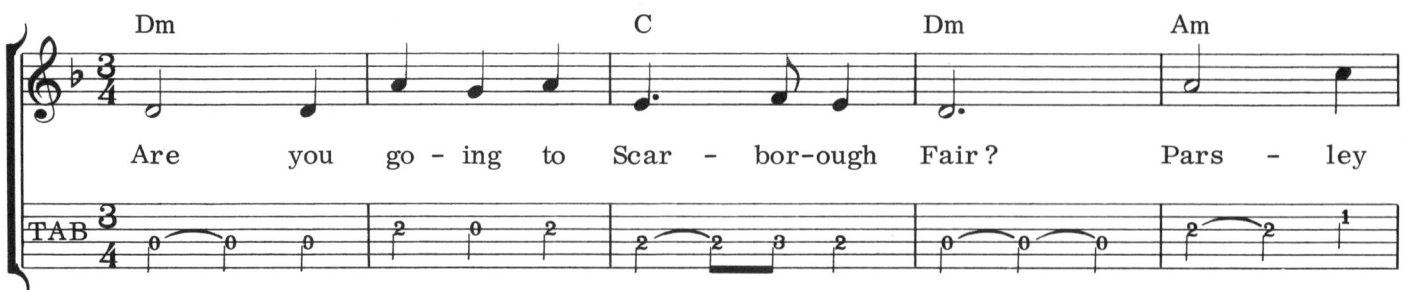

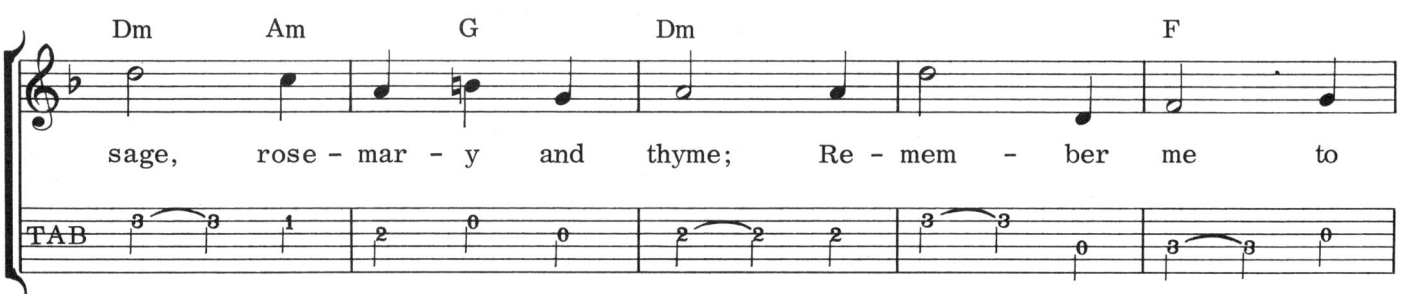

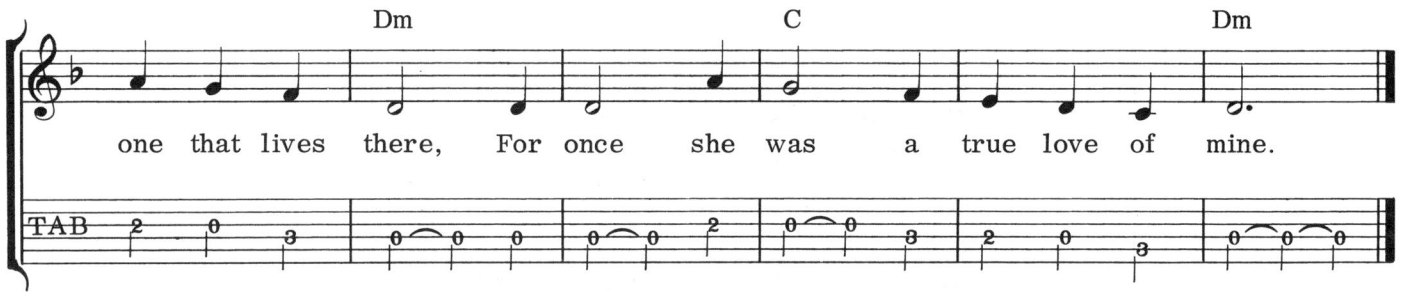

Tell her to make me a cambric shirt,
Parsley, sage, rosemary and thyme;
Without any seam or fine needlework,
And then she'll be a true love of mine.

Tell her to wash it in yonder dry well,
Parsley, sage, rosemary and thyme;
Where water ne'er sprung, nor drop of rain fell,
And then she'll be a true love of mine.

Tell her to dry it on yonder thorn,
Parsley, sage, rosemary and thyme;
Which never bore blossom since Adam was born,
And then she'll be a true love of mine.

Oh, will you find me an acre of land,
Parsley, sage, rosemary and thyme;
Between the sea foam and the sea sand?
Or never be a true love of mine.

Oh, will you plough it with a lamb's horn,
Parsley, sage, rosemary and thyme;
And sow it all over with one peppercorn?
Or never be a true love of mine.

Oh, will you reap it with a sickle of leather,
Parsley, sage, rosemary and thyme;
And tie it all up with a peacock's feather?
Or never be a true love of mine.

And when you have done and finished your work,
Parsley, sage, rosemary and thyme;
Then come to me for your cambric shirt,
And you shall be a true love of mine.

RAILROAD BILL — A NEW G7 CHORD

You should review the first version of *Railroad Bill* in the previous chapter before attempting this arrangement which is more difficult. The new G7 chord (shown in Figures 116 and 117 in the Chord Analysis Box) adds the little finger. This inversion of the G7 chord gives a different sound to the bass line and is quite useful in certain styles of fingerpicking. (It is often used by Elizabeth Cotton and Gary Davis, for example.)

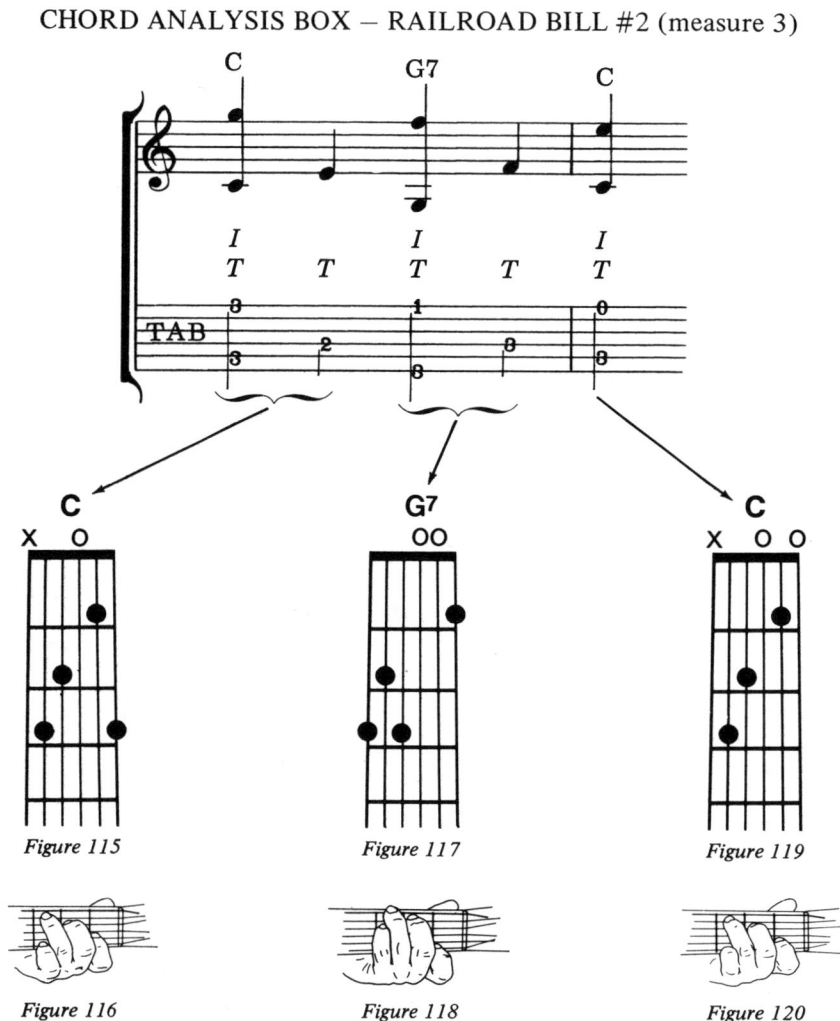

Figure 115 Figure 117 Figure 119

Figure 116 Figure 118 Figure 120

Railroad Bill-Solo

BULLY OF THE TOWN

This song in the key of C uses a long A chord, a D chord, and a C# chord in addition to the expected C, F, and G7 chords. The C# chord is fingered simply by moving the entire C chord up one fret as clearly illustrated in the Chord Analysis Box.

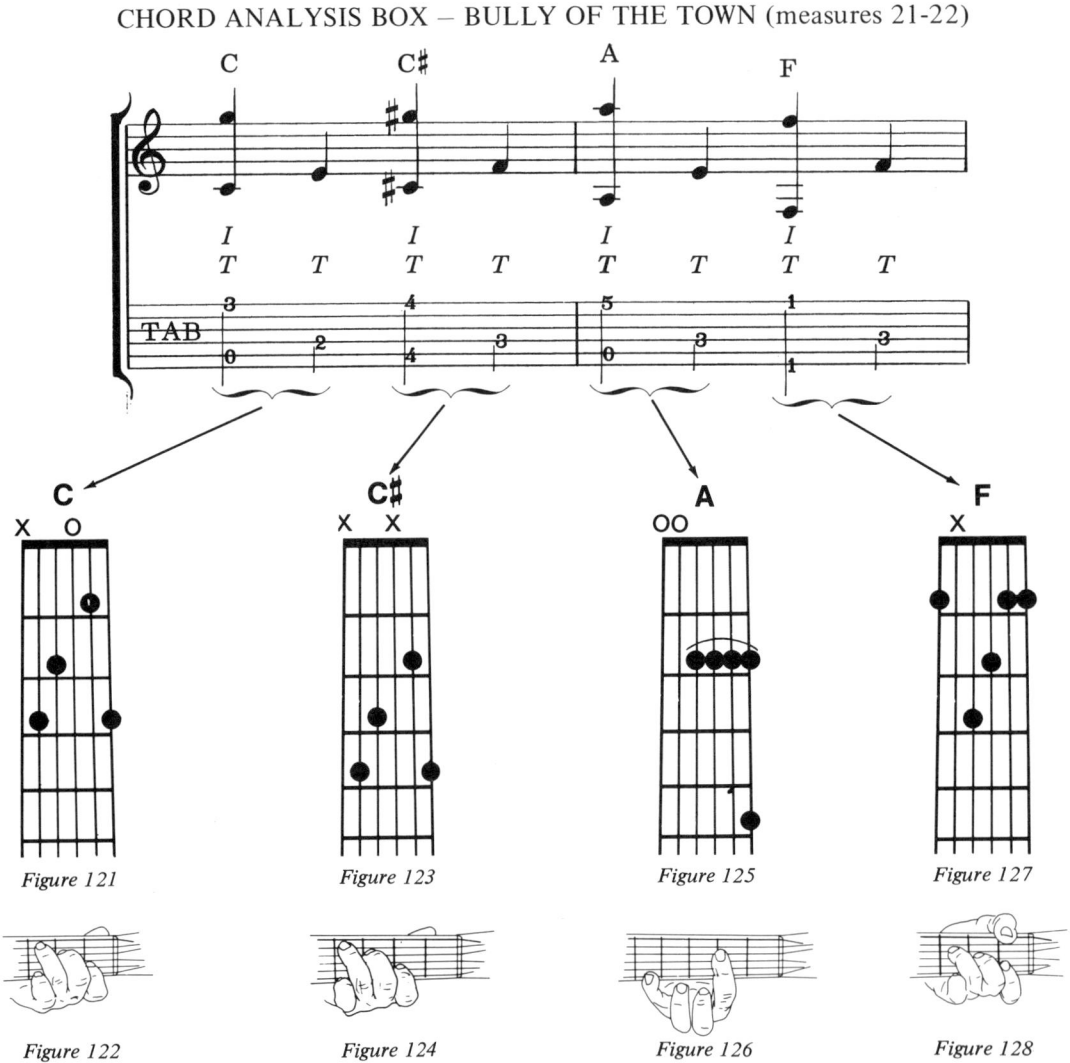

Figure 121   *Figure 123*   *Figure 125*   *Figure 127*

Figure 122   *Figure 124*   *Figure 126*   *Figure 128*

In the 2nd measure, we encounter a variation of the C chord known as a C augmented 9th chord or simply C + 9.

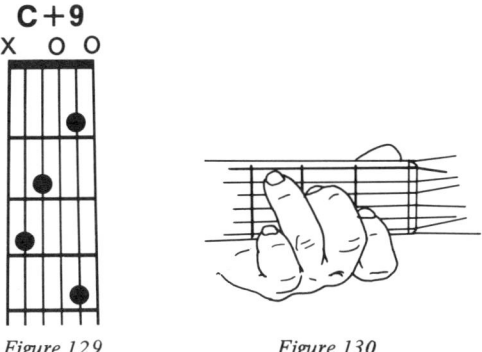

Figure 129   Figure 130

The movement from the C chord in measure 4 to the long A in measure 5 is made clear by examining the Chord Analysis Box for those measures.

CHORD ANALYSIS BOX — BULLY OF THE TOWN (measures 3-5)

Figure 131 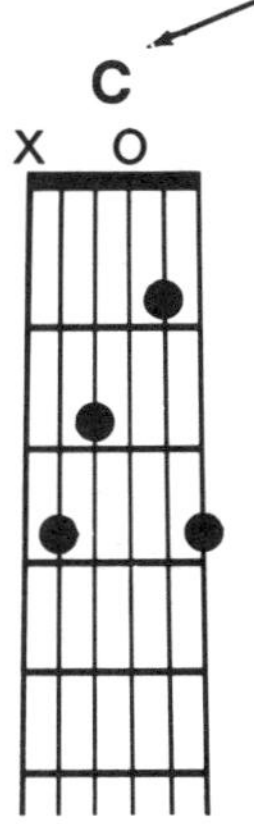   Figure 133    Figure 135 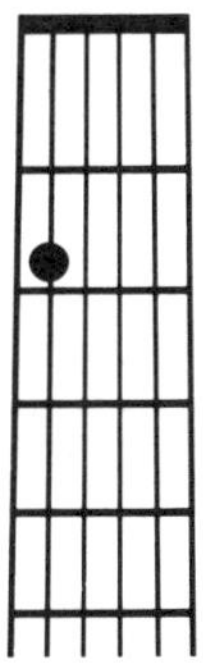   Figure 137 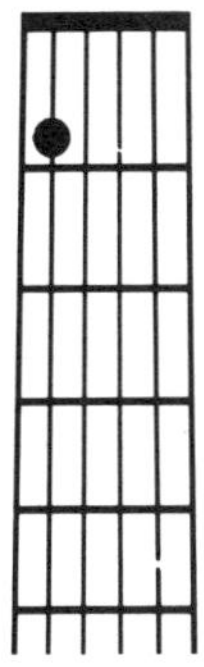   Figure 139    Figure 141

Figure 132    Figure 134    Figure 136 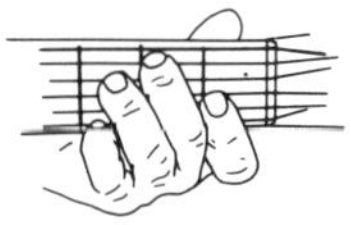   Figure 138 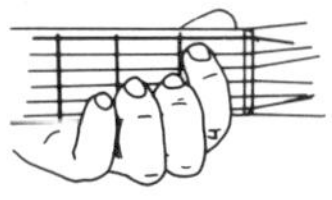   Figure 140 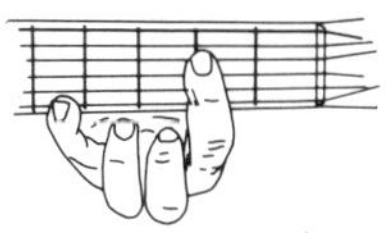   Figure 142

65

Bully of the Town - Solo

HAMMERS AND SLIDES

As our fingerpicking has progressed, you may have noticed that the solos call for more and more notes that do not correspond to the melody lines for the songs. When we began fingerpicking, we simply played the melody notes with a continuous bass line using on-beat pinches. In the last chapter we have supplemented the melody notes with "extraneous" notes to play more interesting solos. We can further embellish the solos with two forms of ornamentation: the *hammer* and the *slide*.

Hammers and slides can be simply described (see Introduction for review). The hammer occurs when the right hand sounds a string, usually open, and the left hand modifies the pitch by fretting the string. Slides are similar to hammers except that the pitch is modified by a movement of the left hand up or down the guitar neck. The pitch is changed by altering the fret position; i.e. the fretting finger slides along the string and across the frets. We will be concerned primarily with a study of the rhythm of various types of hammers and slides.

Once the pitch of the sixth string has been altered, the fingering of the chords using this string must be changed also. The D chord (Figures 144 and 145) now uses all six strings. A good alternating bass is obtained from the open sixth and fourth strings. The G chord (Figures 146 and 147) does not make use of the sixth string. The A (or A7) chord (Figures 148 and 149) retains the same hand position, but again the sixth string is not used. The alternating bass for both the G and A chords in this tuning will be from the fifth to the fourth string.

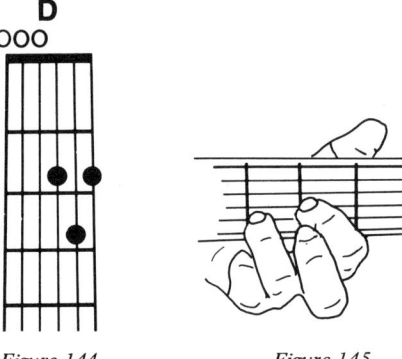

Figure 144   Figure 145

STACKERLEE — SIMPLE HAMMERS

The first song of this chapter, in addition to displaying the use of hammers, uses a new guitar tuning. To make it easier to play in the key of D, the sixth string of the guitar is often lowered from E to D making it possible to use this string in the alternating bass for the D chord. To change from the standard tuning to this tuning, only the sixth string is retuned (Figure 143). The sixth string when fretted at the seventh fret has the same pitch as the fifth string open.

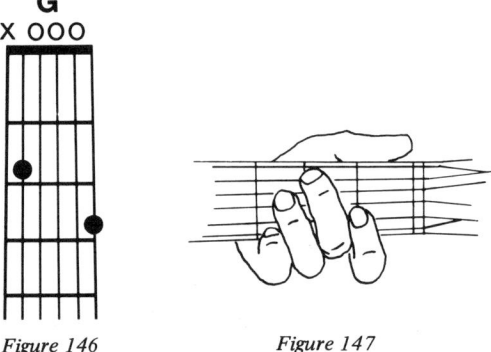

Figure 146   Figure 147

Figure 143

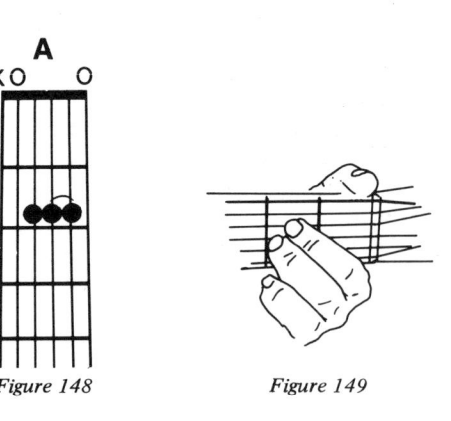

Figure 148   Figure 149

Once you are familiar with these chord positions, go on to the solo version of *Stackerlee*. The Chord Analysis Box for measure 1 illustrates the hammer. This should not prove difficult since the rhythm is identical to that used in Carter-style picking. The Chord Analysis Box for the 8th measure illustrates how three descending notes on the top string form a D to Dm chord progression. The Chord Analysis Box for the 9th measure shows the technique for a simple slide: play the A♭ chord (Figures 164 and 165) then, without releasing the pressure holding the strings down, slide your fingers into the A chord position (Figures 166 and 167). The rhythm is the same as in the hammer.

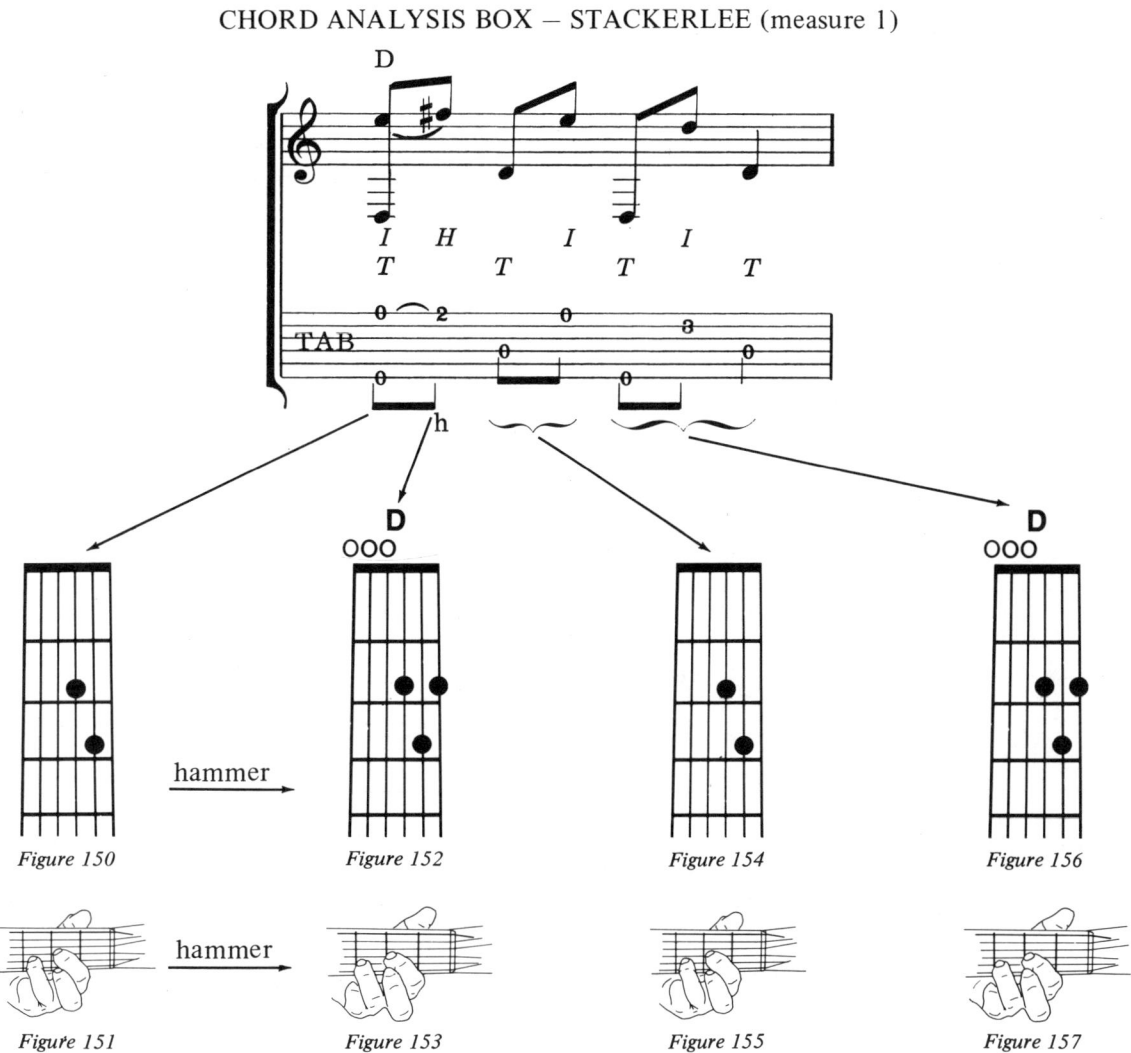

CHORD ANALYSIS BOX — STACKERLEE (measure 1)

Figure 150

Figure 151

Figure 152

Figure 153

Figure 154

Figure 155

Figure 156

Figure 157

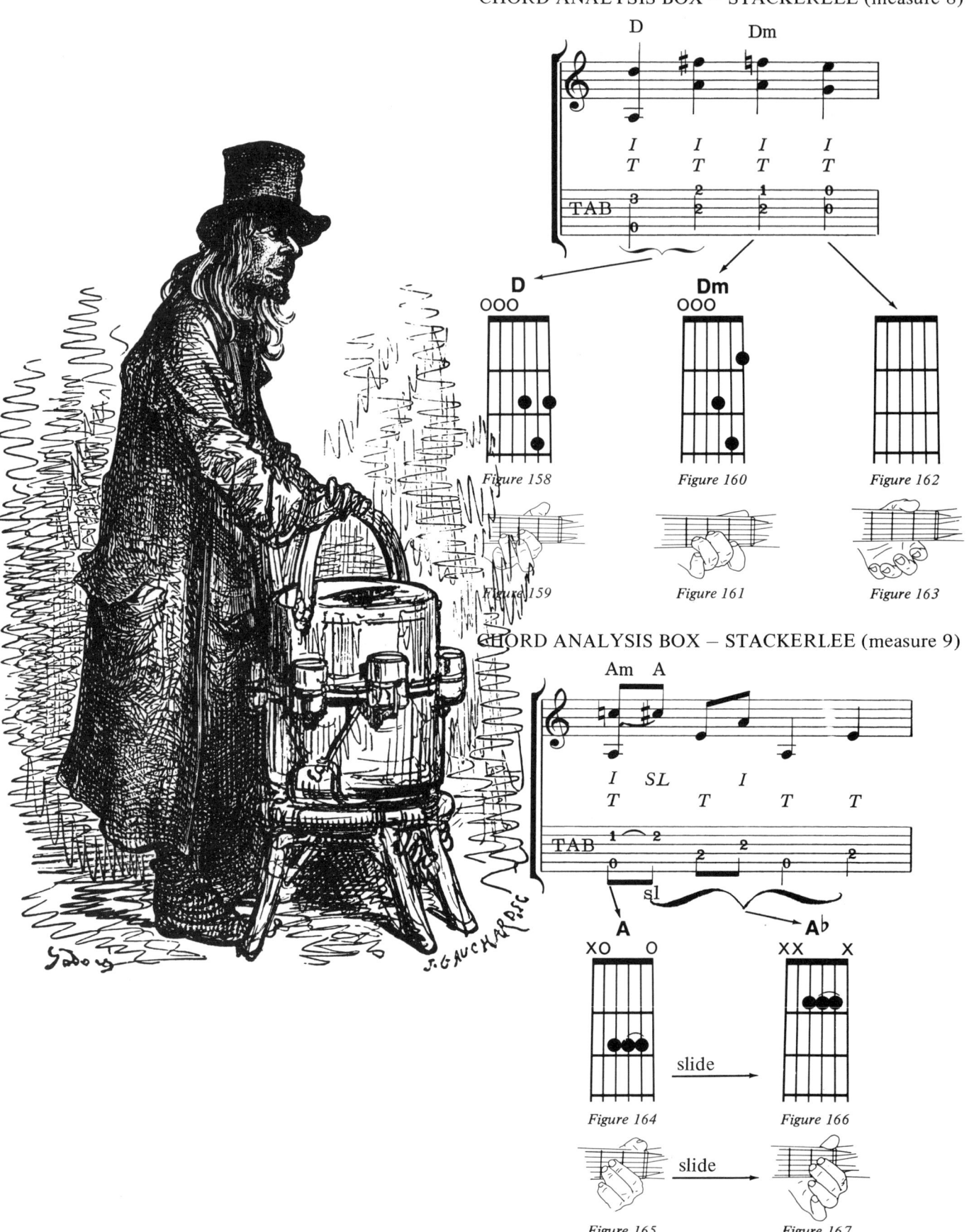

CHORD ANALYSIS BOX – STACKERLEE (measure 8)

Figure 158
Figure 160
Figure 162

Figure 159
Figure 161
Figure 163

CHORD ANALYSIS BOX – STACKERLEE (measure 9)

Figure 164
Figure 166

Figure 165
Figure 167

Stackerlee-Solo

Stackerlee-Melody

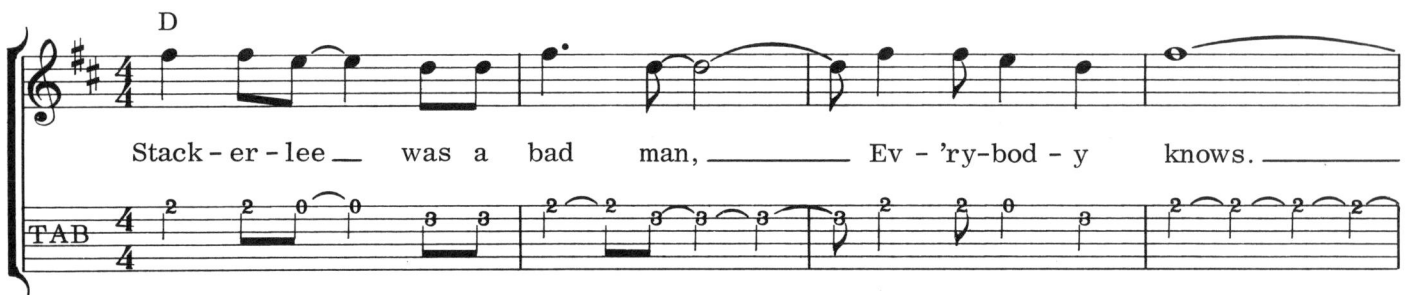
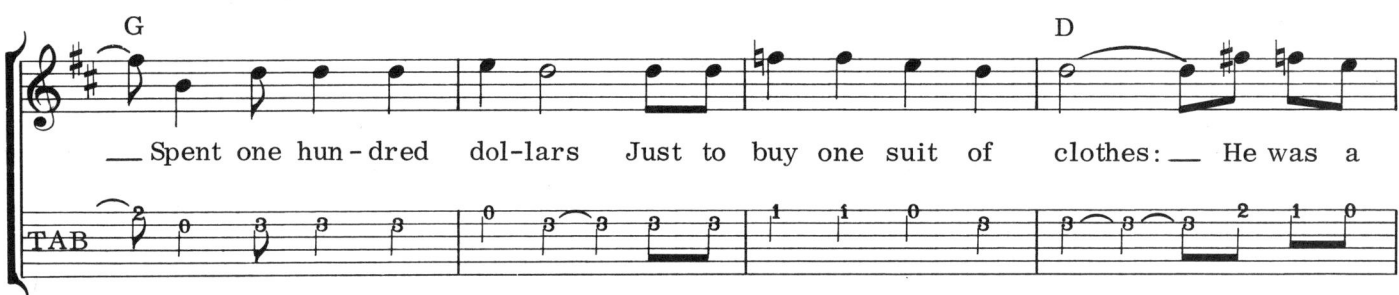

Stackerlee shot Billy Lyon,
What do you think about that?
Shot him down in cold blood
'Cause he stole his Stetson hat:
He was a bad man
That mean old Stackerlee.

Billy Lyon said, "Stackerlee,
Please don't take my life,
I've got two little children
And a darling, loving wife,
You are a bad man,
Mean old Stackerlee."

"God'll take care of your children,
And I'll take care of your wife –
You done stole my Stetson hat
And I'm gonna take your life."
He was a bad man,
Mean old Stackerlee.

There's a place down in New Orleans
They call the Lyon's Club.
And every step that you step,
You step in Billy Lyon's blood.
He was a bad man,
Mean old Stackerlee.

RAILROAD BILL #2 — OFF-BEAT HAMMERS

Look over the music to *Railroad Bill* and you will see that for the E chord (5th measure) a new pattern is used. It involves a hammer that is different from the one we learned for Carter-style picking. Finger-picking commonly uses what is called the *off-beat hammer*. This figure begins with the sounding of the open string between the beats and the hammered note is sounded on the following beat. This will become clear as we work through the examples below.

Let us begin by assembling the off-beat hammer bit by bit. Finger an E chord and play the music in Figures 168. The index finger, *not the thumb,* is used to pick the third string open. So far we have nothing but a simple hammer.

Figure 168

In the next example (Figure 169) the index fingers of both hands do *exactly* the same thing as in Figure 168. However, as you hammer with the index finger, the thumb of the right hand sounds the sixth string open. The hammered note and the bass note should sound like a pinched note. The third string open is sounded on the "&" before the beat while the bass note and the hammer are sounded on the beat itself. The bass note should not be so loud as to drown out the hammered note.

Figure 169

In the third example (Figure 170), a thumb note has been added to the beginning of the hammer figure. This thumb note corresponds to the second beat of the measure, thus the count of this example is "2 & 3." Remember to hold down the entire E chord while playing these examples.

Figure 170

In Figure 171, the fourth example, the second string open is to be played by the index finger of the right hand following the completion of the hammered figure. This note comes after the third beat of the measure and extends the count to "2 & 3 &."

Figure 171

In the final example (Figure 172), the off-beat hammer is completed by adding a pinch on the first beat and a final thumb note on the last beat. The rhythm of the whole measure is "1, 2 &, 3 &, 4." Be sure that the rhythm is even. The hammered note must coincide exactly with the thumb note on the third beat.

Figure 172

Railroad Bill 2-Solo

TOM DOOLEY — HAMMERS IN C AND G

Off-beat hammers using C and G chords are more difficult than the one you just learned. This is because the hammering finger must move from one string to another in the course of the hammer.

The Chord Analysis Box corresponding to the 1st measure of *Tom Dooley* illustrates the hammer while holding the C chord. The second finger must move from the fourth string to hammer on the second fret of the third string (Figures 175 and 176). Do not forget to return this finger to its original position (Figures 177 and 178) or the bass notes will not be correct.

The second Chord Analysis Box, corresponding to the 5th measure, illustrates a hammer technique possible with the G chord. This again is on the third string. In this chord, hammers also occur on the fourth and second strings.

CHORD ANALYSIS BOX — TOM DOOLEY (measure 1)

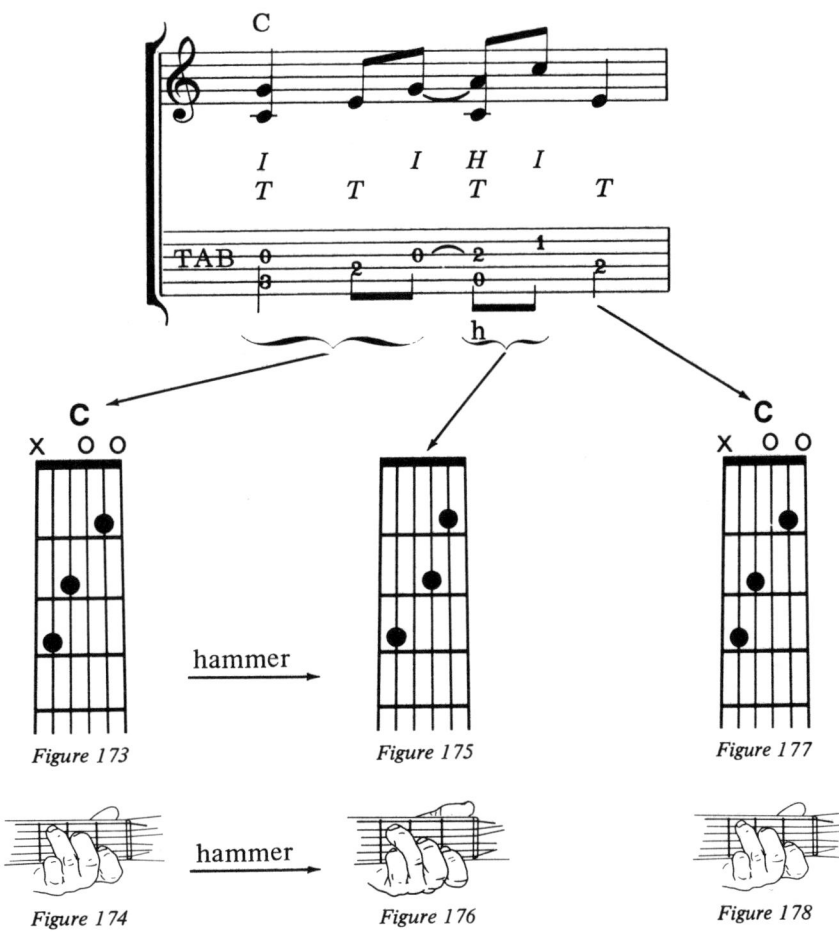

Figure 173   *Figure 175*   *Figure 177*

Figure 174   *Figure 176*   *Figure 178*

CHORD ANALYSIS BOX – TOM DOOLEY (measure 5)

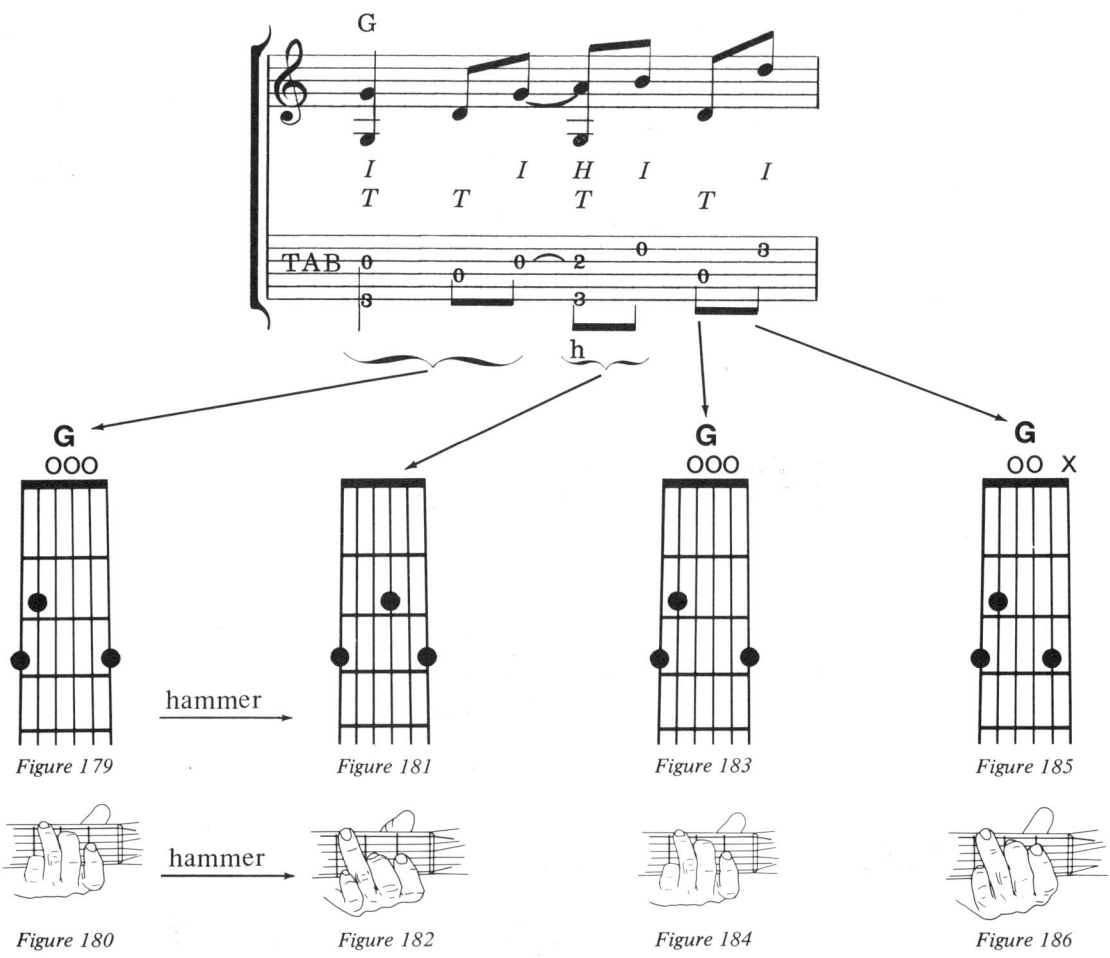

Figure 179
Figure 180
Figure 181
Figure 182
Figure 183
Figure 184
Figure 185
Figure 186

hammer

Tom Dooley-Solo

FREIGHT TRAIN – HAMMERS IN F

We will now use a simplified version of Elizabeth Cotton's *Freight Train* to illustrate the technique of the hammer while holding the F chord position. The Chord Analysis Box for measure 12 illustrates the necessary hand positions. Though there is a similarity between the hammer in F and the one in E, the F chord is more difficult to finger during the hammer. A little practice will conquer this difficulty.

The second Chord Analysis Box (for measures 13 and 14) illustrates the same F chord hammer used in a slightly different way.

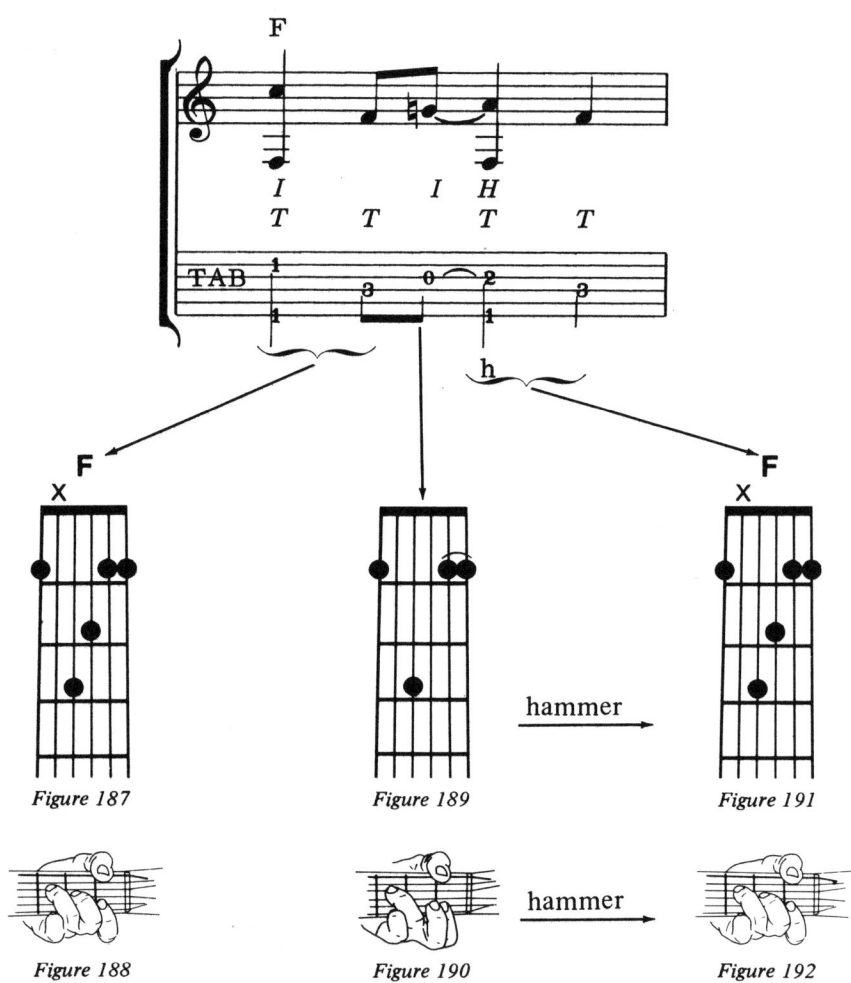

CHORD ANALYSIS BOX – FREIGHT TRAIN (measure 12)

Figure 187   *Figure 189*   *Figure 191*

Figure 188   *Figure 190*   *Figure 192*

CHORD ANALYSIS BOX – FREIGHT TRAIN (measures 13-14)

Figure 193 Figure 195 Figure 197 Figure 199

Figure 194 Figure 196 Figure 198 Figure 200

Freight Train-Solo

by Elizabeth Cotton

Freight Train-Melody

by Elizabeth Cotton

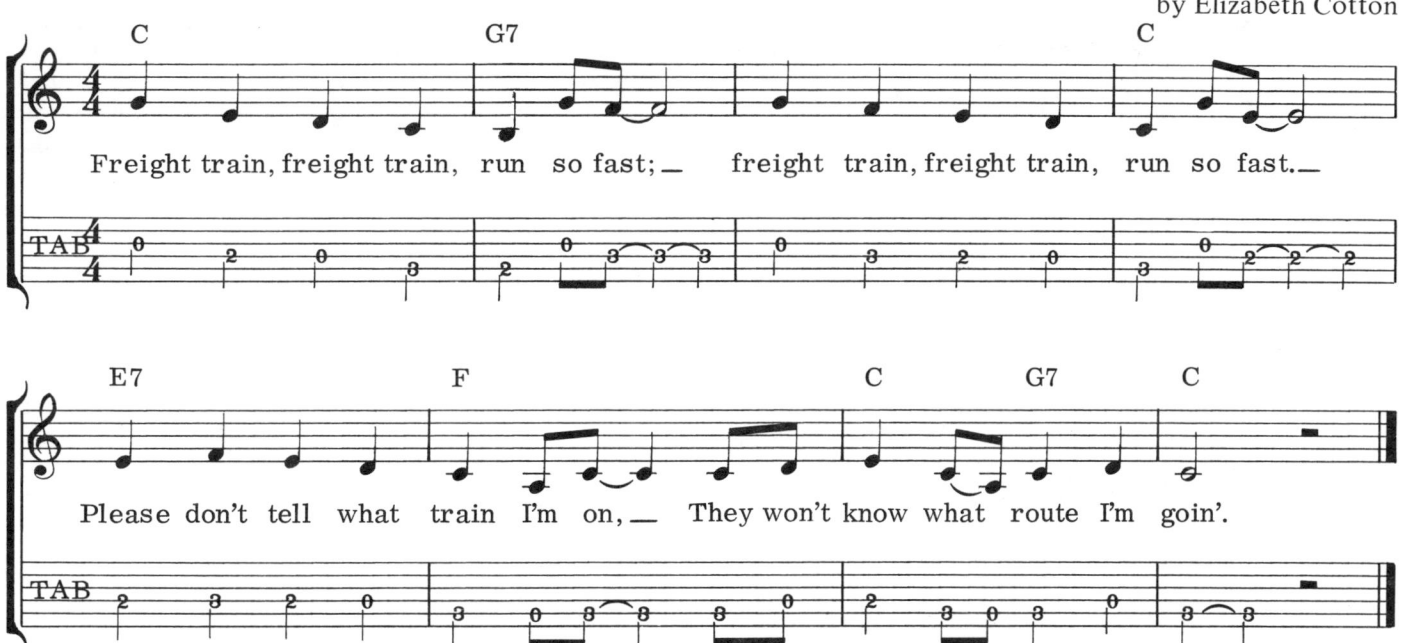

Freight train, freight train, run so fast;_ freight train, freight train, run so fast._

Please don't tell what train I'm on,_ They won't know what route I'm goin'.

When I'm dead and in my grave,
No more good times here I crave;
Place the stones at my head and feet,
And tell them all that I've gone to sleep.

When I die, Lord, bury me deep,
Way down on old Chestnut Street,
So I can hear old Number Nine
As she goes rolling by.

When I die, Lord, bury me deep,
Way down on old Chestnut Street;
Place the stones at my head and feet,
And tell them all that I'm gone to sleep.

FREIGHT TRAIN #2 — THE REAL THING

The last version of *Freight Train* was simplified for instructional purposes. Most of the solos in this collection were not intended for performance nor are they notations of the performance of others. To give the student some idea of an original, note-for-note notation of a guitar solo, the following version of *Freight Train* is included.

The greatest difficulty with exact notations is that the performances of the songs tend to be complex. Most guitarists do not record simplified solos because they want to be heard at their best. Thus the student must contend with solos that may have taken a lifetime to develop. Accurate notations of performed solos are available in other books such as Don Garwood's *Masters of Instrumental Blues Guitar*, Happy Traum's *Finger-Picking Styles for Guitar*, and Stefan Grossman's *Country Blues Guitar* (all Oak Publications).

The C chord used in *Freight Train* (Figures 201 and 202) is a modification of the C chord we already know. Notice that the bass line in this C chord must be changed from a fifth string-fourth string to a *sixth* string-fourth string alternating bass. The sixth-string bass is used almost throughout the song. The hammer into the E chord should not be difficult after learning the hammers in the preceding version of *Freight Train*. The second set of hammers, shown in the Chord Analysis Box for measures 13 and 14, is similar to the one we learned for the G chord in *Tom Dooley*.

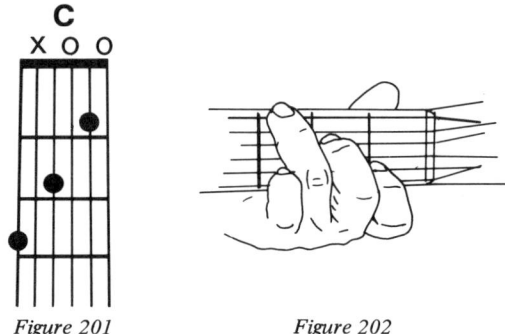

Figure 201 Figure 202

CHORD ANALYSIS BOX — FREIGHT TRAIN #2 (measures 13 and 14)

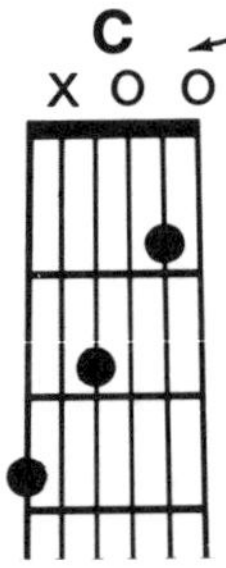

Figure 203 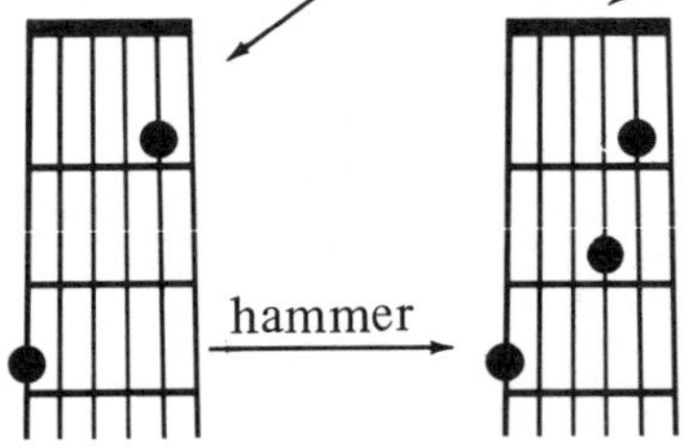 Figure 205 Figure 207 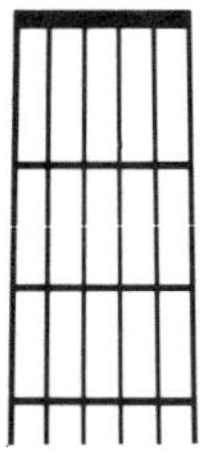 Figure 209 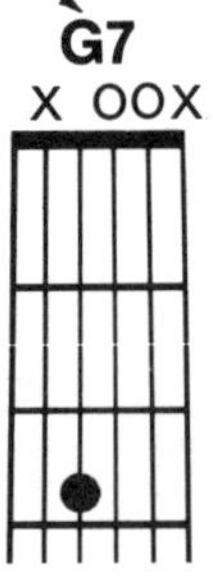 Figure 211  Figure 213

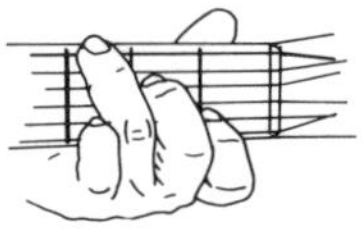

Figure 204 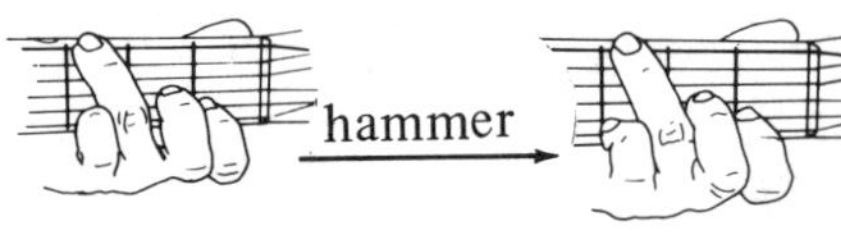 Figure 206 Figure 208  Figure 210 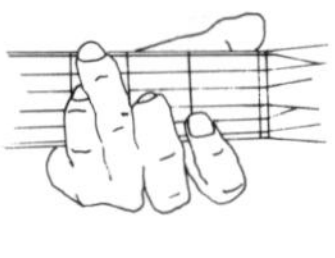 Figure 212  Figure 214

82

Freight Train 2-Solo

by Elizabeth Cotton

ONE DIME BLUES — SLIDES

The slide is a form of ornamentation which is closely related to the hammer. It is commonly used in fingerpicking. A string is picked at a specific fret then, without releasing the pressure on the string, the fretting finger slides up (or down) the guitar neck. This changes the pitch of the note being played with little loss of volume. The sound produced is distinctly different from the hammer. Slides are indicated in the music and tablature by a tie above the notes and the letters "sl."

The rhythm of slides can be either on-beat or off-beat similar to hammers. *One Dime Blues* contains several examples of on-beat slides. The slide in the 1st measure is detailed in the Chord Analysis Box. Notice that the same finger positions is moved up several frets though some of the notes are not picked at each position (Figures 217 and 219). These notes will sound because of the slide. In the second Chord Analysis Box (13th and 14th measures) the entire figure is played using only one basic fingering position. Tricks such as these considerably simplify many fingerpicking songs.

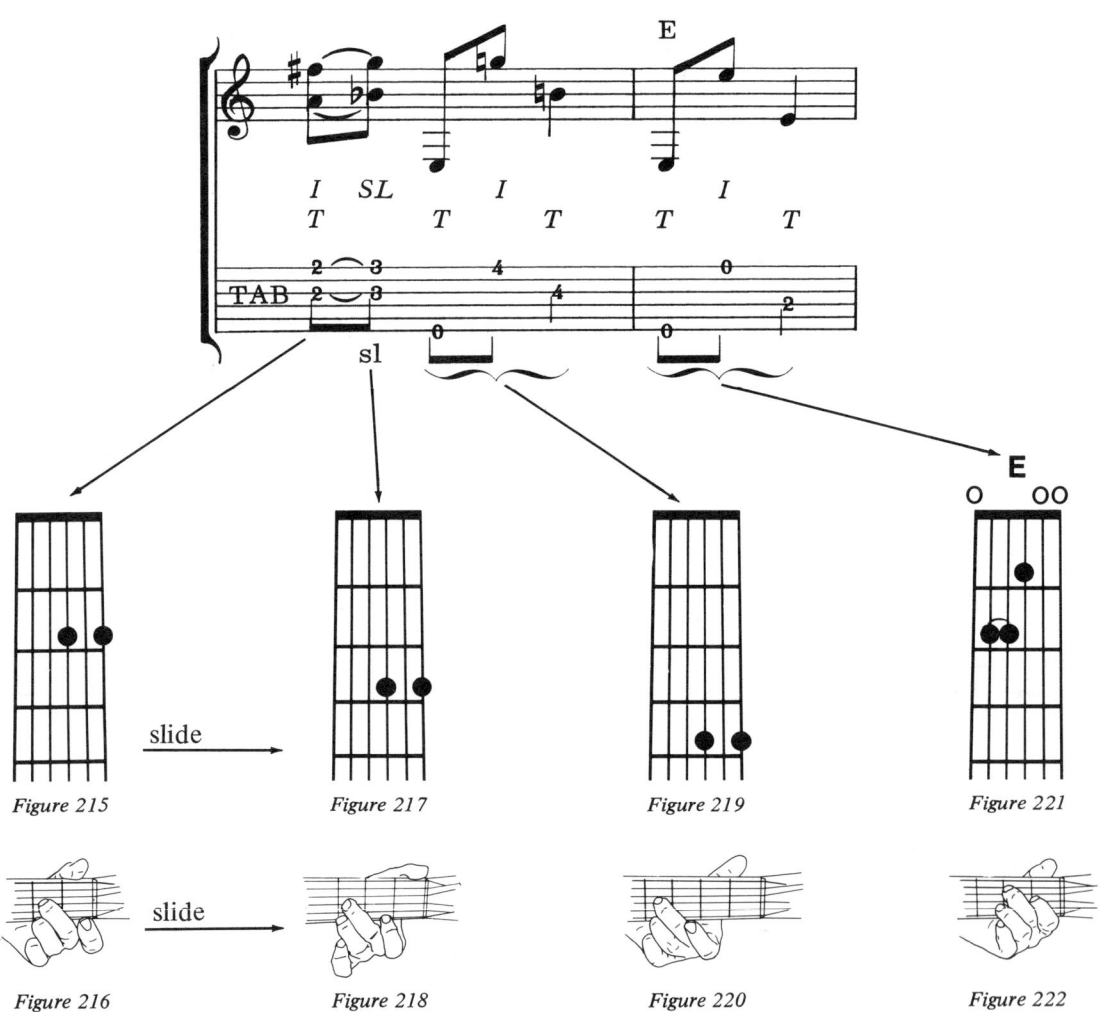

CHORD ANALYSIS BOX — ONE DIME BLUES (measure 1)

Figure 215 *Figure 217* *Figure 219* *Figure 221*

Figure 216 *Figure 218* *Figure 220* *Figure 222*

CHORD ANALYSIS BOX — ONE DIME BLUES (measures 10-11)

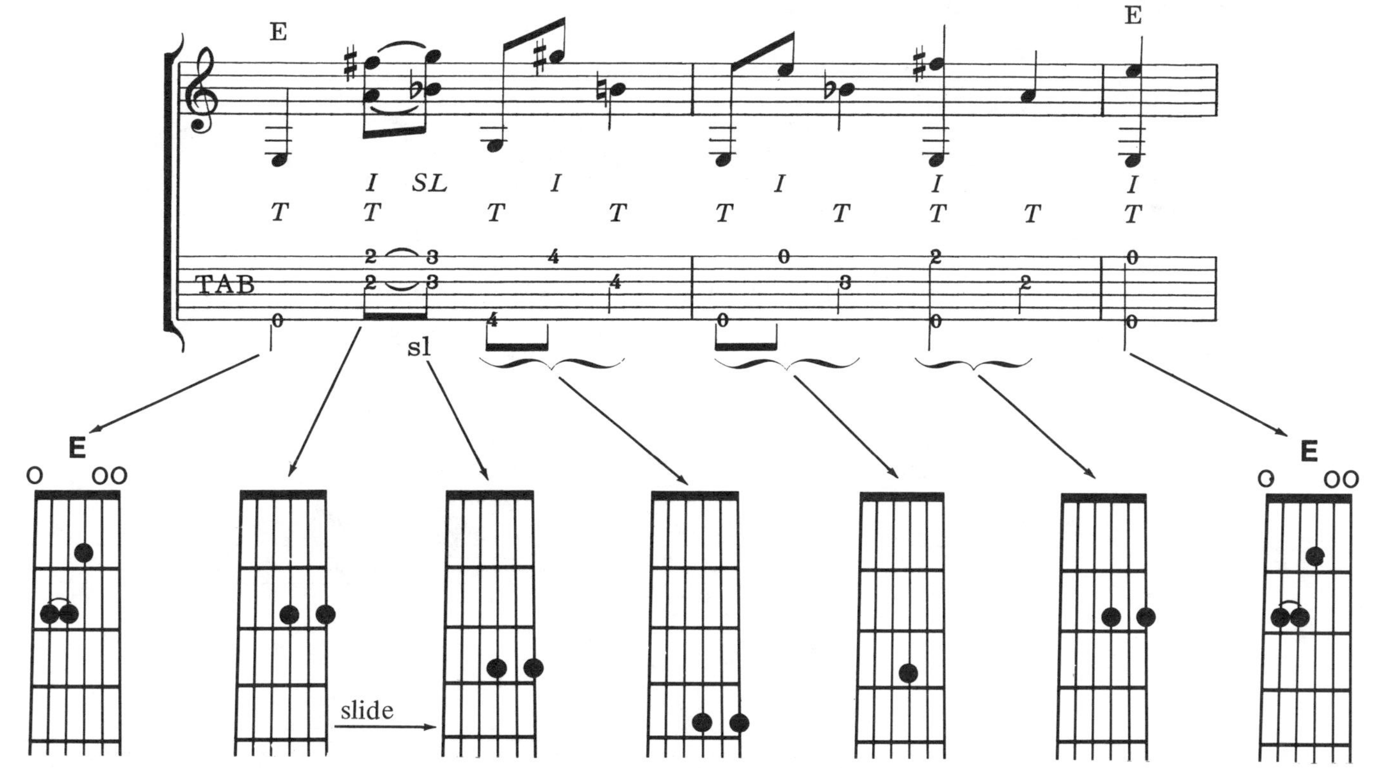

Figure 223   Figure 225   Figure 227   Figure 229   Figure 231   Figure 233   Figure 235

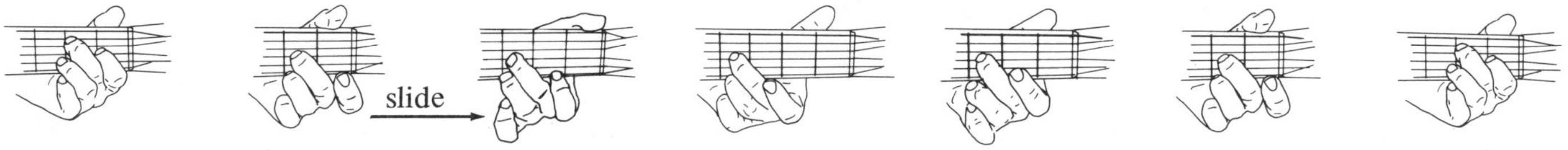

Figure 224   Figure 226   Figure 228   Figure 230   Figure 232   Figure 234   Figure 236

One Dime Blues-Solo

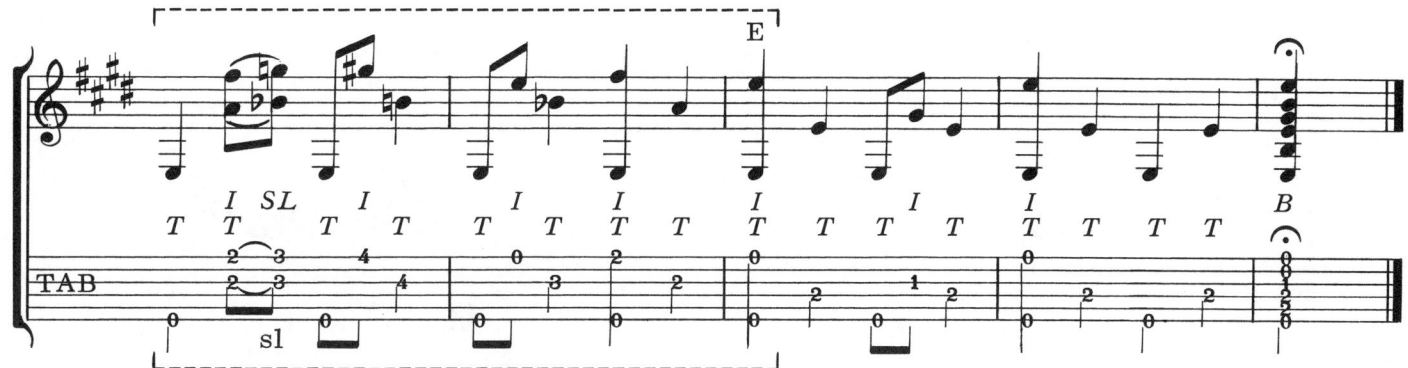

One Dime Blues-Melody

I came down from East St. Louis, Now I

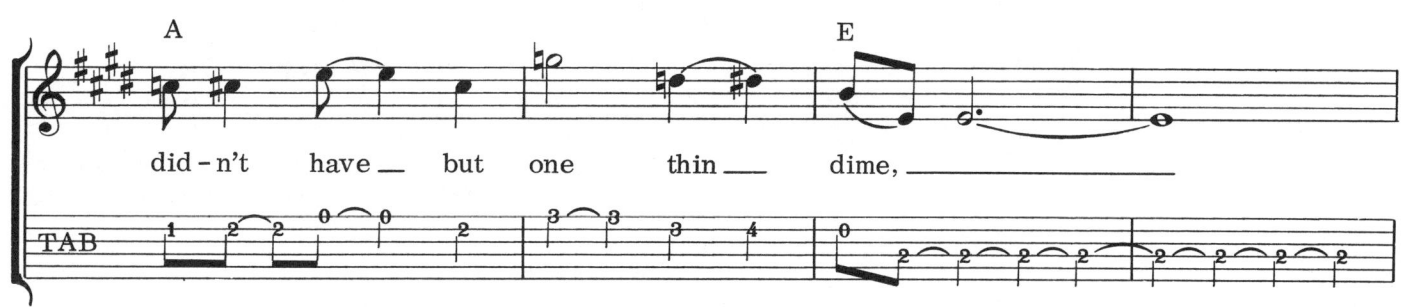

did-n't have but one thin dime,

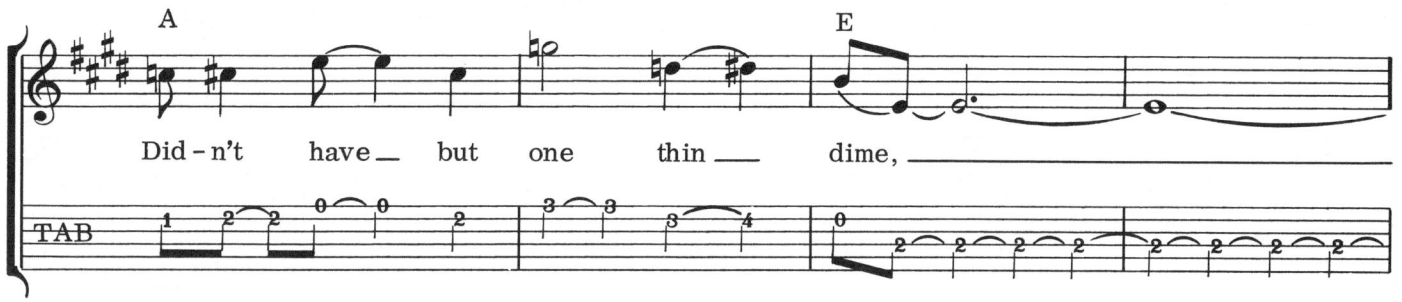

Did-n't have but one thin dime,

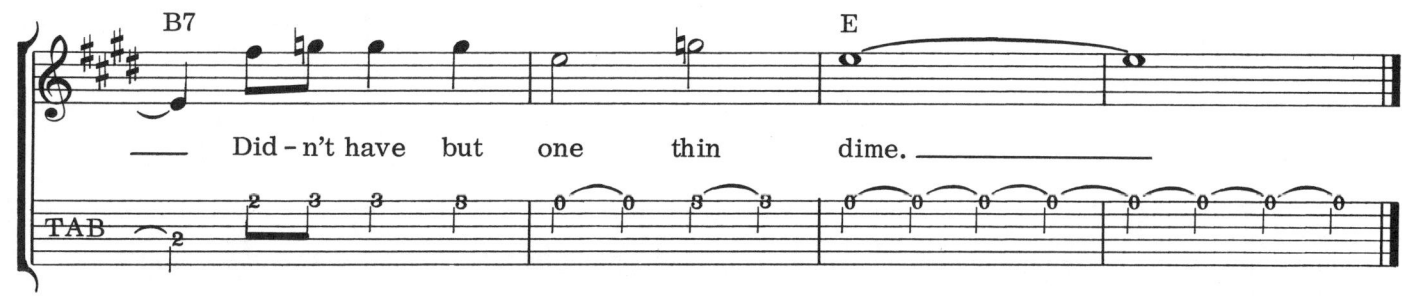

Did-n't have but one thin dime.

SALTY DOG — COMBINED HAMMERS AND SLIDES

We are now ready to combine hammers and slides. In *Salty Dog* we have hammers in the chords E and D, and a slide in the A chord. The hammer in E should be familiar from several of the previous songs (see Figure 172 in *Railroad Bill*). The hammer in D is similar to the one used at the beginning of this chapter in *Stackerlee* (see figures 150 to 153). The slide in the A chord uses the A position outlined in the Chord Analysis Box for *Stackerlee* (Figures 164 to 167). The difficulties in *Salty Dog* arise not from the techniques, but from their combination.

Salty Dog-Solo

Salty Dog-Melody

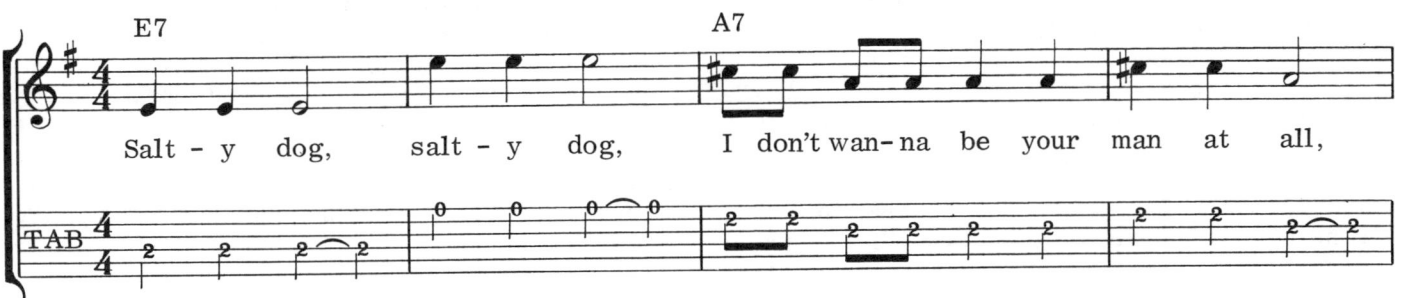

God made a woman, He made her kinda funny,
Kiss her 'round her mouth, tastes just like honey.
Honey let me be your salty dog.

Worst day I had in my life,
When my boss caught me kissing his wife.
Honey, let me be your salty dog.

Little fish, big fish, swimmin' in the water,
Come back here, man, and marry my daughter.
Honey, let me be your salty dog.

I got a nickel, I got a dime,
If you shake yours, I'll shake mine.
Honey, let me be your salty dog.

SALTY DOG #2 — COMPLEX HAMMERS AND SLIDES

This more complex version of *Salty Dog* includes hammers in long A, slides and hammers in D, and a hammer in G. Notice that the two hammers at the second and third frets are different even though they are for the same chord. The hammer in the 3rd measure is an on-beat hammer, while that in the 4th is an off-beat. The on-beat hammer is outlined in the Chord Analysis Box. Once this is mastered, the second hammer should not be difficult. It is important that the barre for the long A chord properly fret all four strings as shown in Figures 239 and 240.

The second Chord Analysis Box describes the slide and the hammer in the D chord. Note that the slide is on-beat, while the hammer begins on the off-beat.

The off-beat hammer on the G chord in the 7th and 8th measures should also not be difficult. The hammering is done with the index finger of the left hand.

CHORD ANALYSIS BOX — SALTY DOG #2 (measure 3)

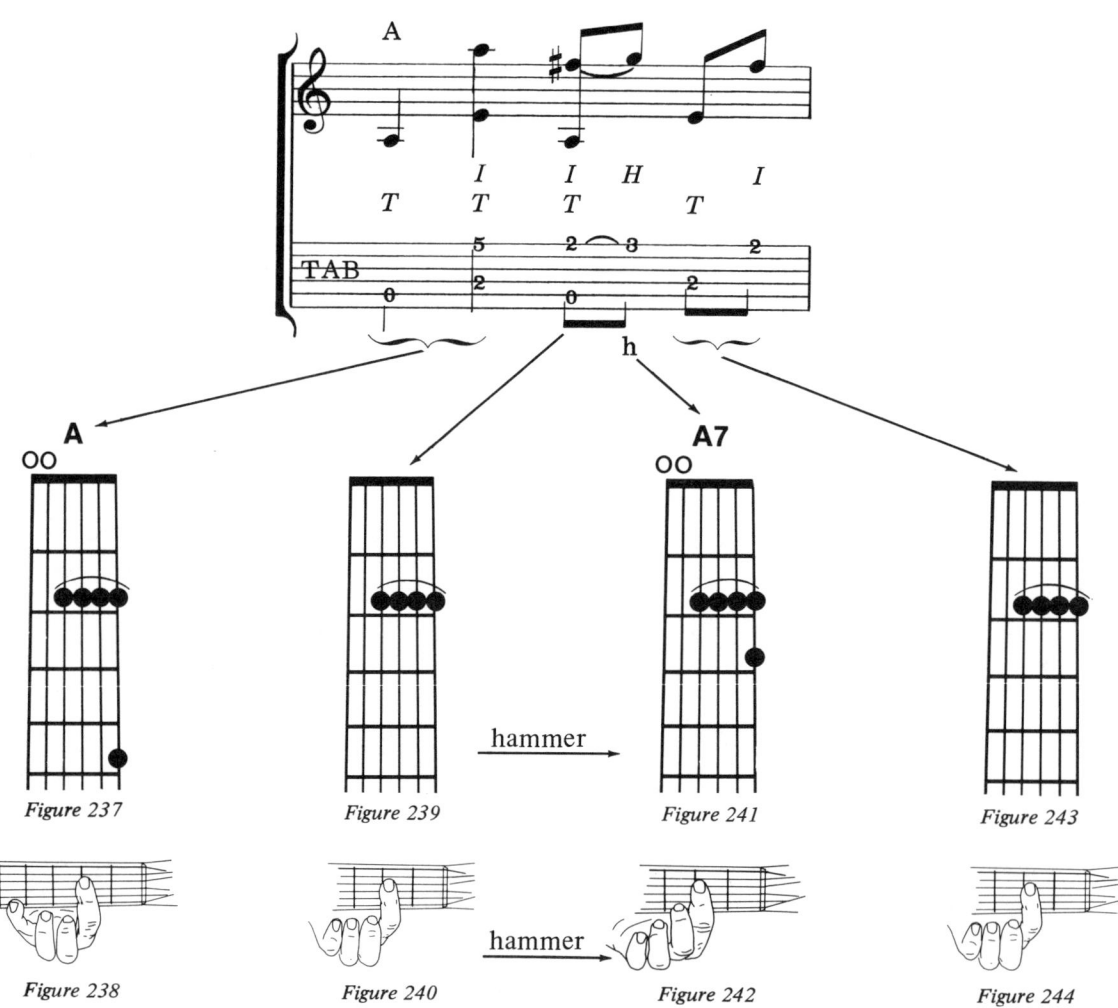

Figure 237

Figure 239

Figure 241

Figure 243

Figure 238

Figure 240

Figure 242

Figure 244

90

CHORD ANALYSIS BOX – SALTY DOG #2 (measure 5)

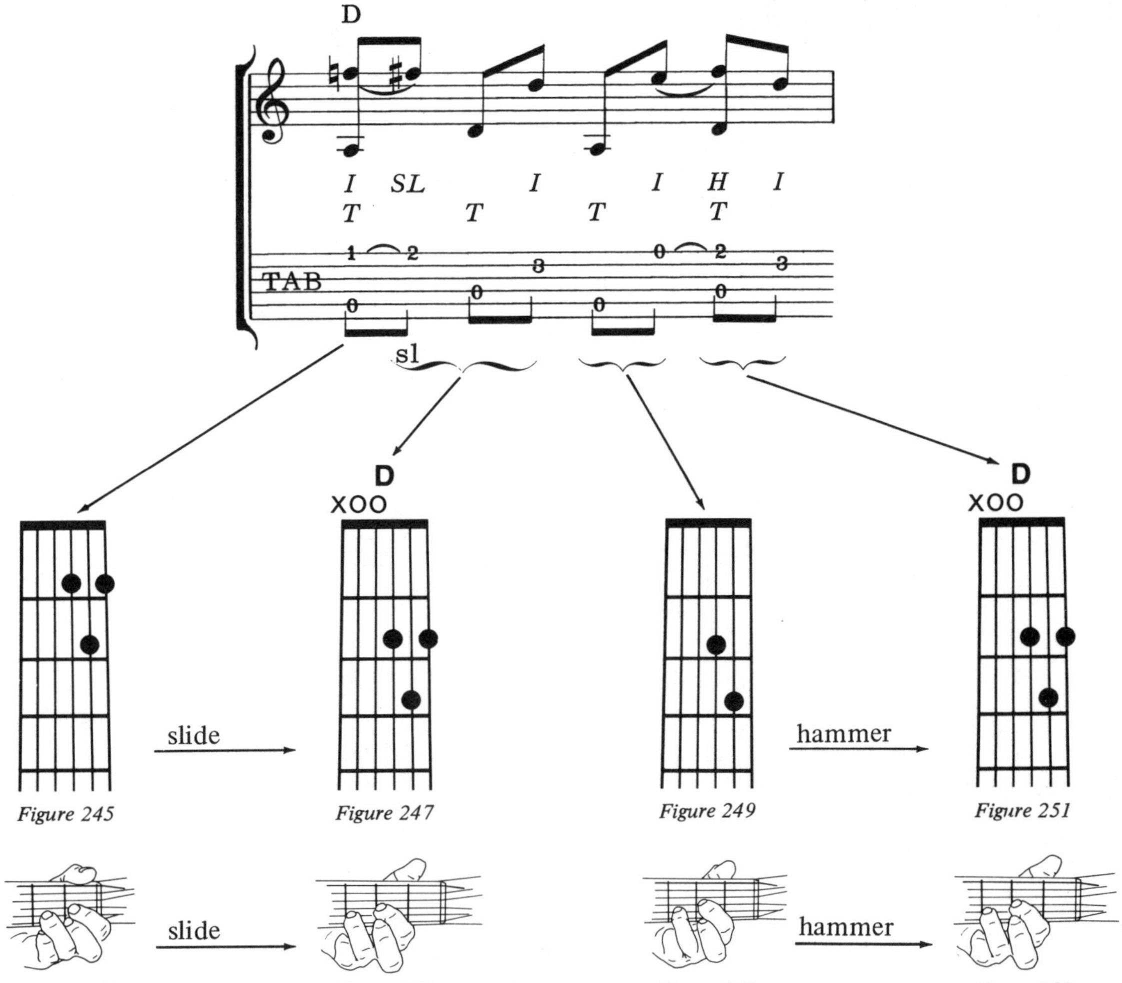

Figure 245 — slide → *Figure 247* | *Figure 249* — hammer → *Figure 251*

Figure 246 — slide → *Figure 248* | *Figure 250* — hammer → *Figure 252*

Salty Dog 2 - Solo

Salty Dog 2 - Melody

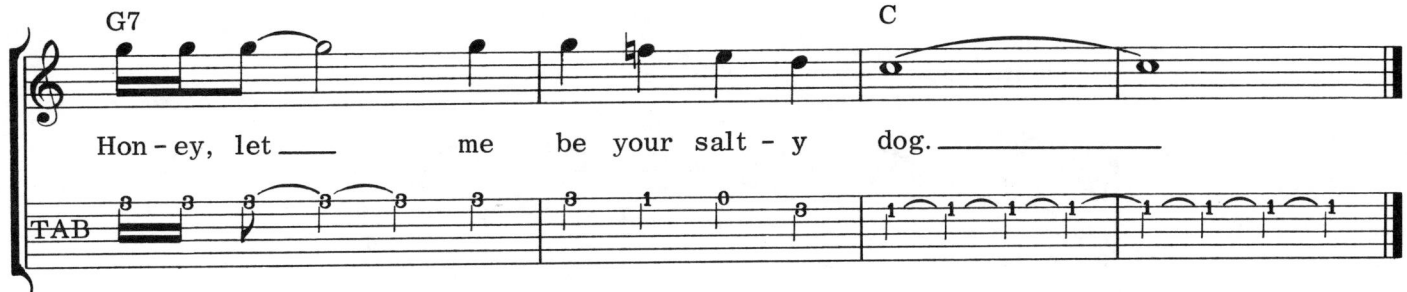

SEE SEE RIDER — OFF-BEAT SLIDES AND PICKS

This song serves as a summary of the various techniques we learned in this chapter. In addition, two new ornaments are introduced. The first is the off-beat slide. This type of slide begins on the off-beat and ends on the beat. The finger positions for this slide are indicated in the Chord Analysis Box for measures 4 and 5.

The second new technique used in *See See Rider* is the pick. The pick can be considered the reverse of the hammer. Here the first note of the figure is sounded by the right hand, while the left hand is holding a fretted note. The finger of the left hand is then quickly removed from the fingerboard with a sideways motion so as to sound the open string. This type of figure is indicated in the music and tablature by a slur mark and the letter "P." Remember that the rhythm of the pick is the same as that of the hammer or the slide.

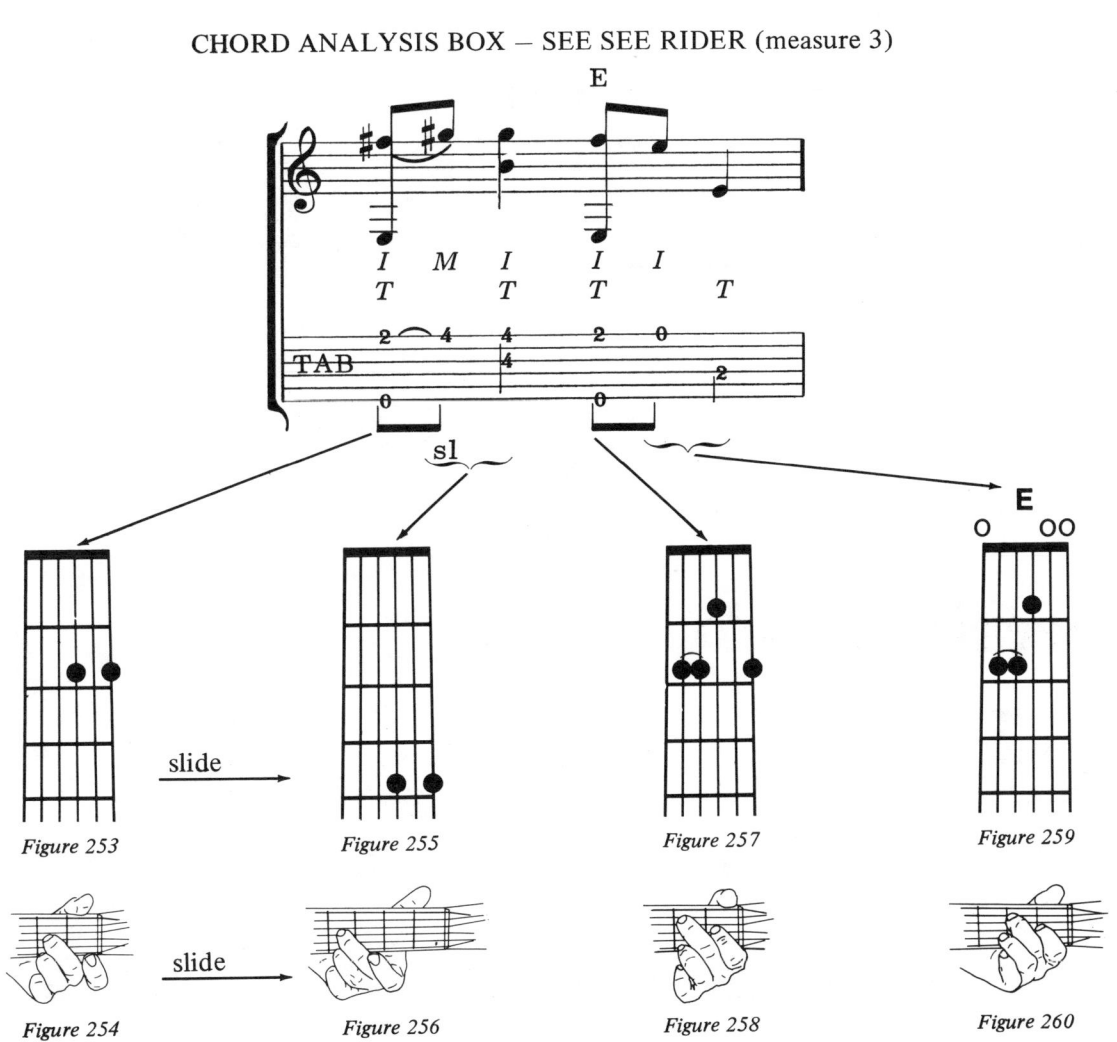

Figure 253 *Figure 255* *Figure 257* *Figure 259*

Figure 254 *Figure 256* *Figure 258* *Figure 260*

CHORD ANALYSIS BOX – SEE SEE RIDER (measures 4-5)

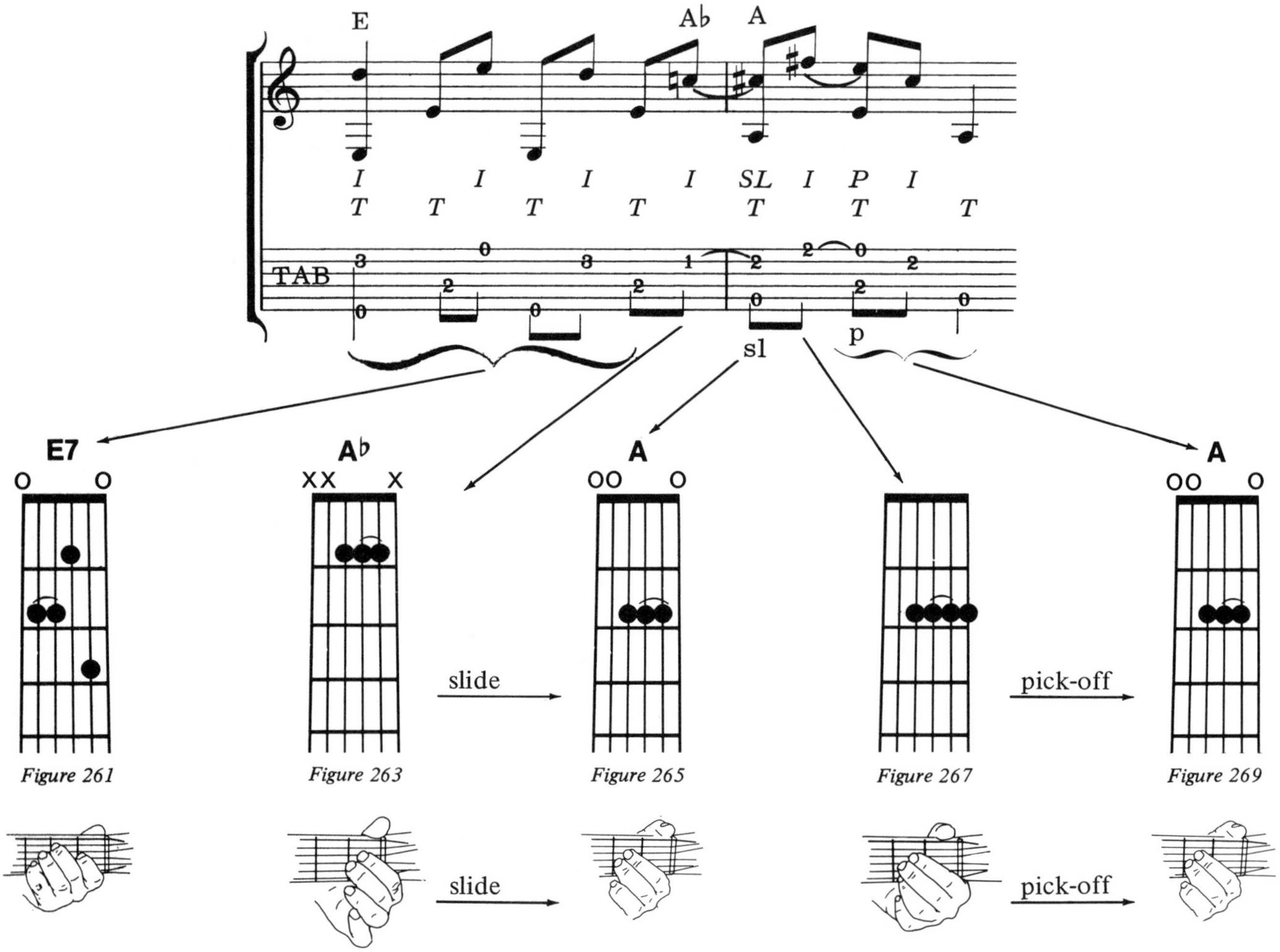

Figure 261 Figure 263 Figure 265 Figure 267 Figure 269

Figure 262 Figure 264 Figure 266 Figure 268 Figure 270

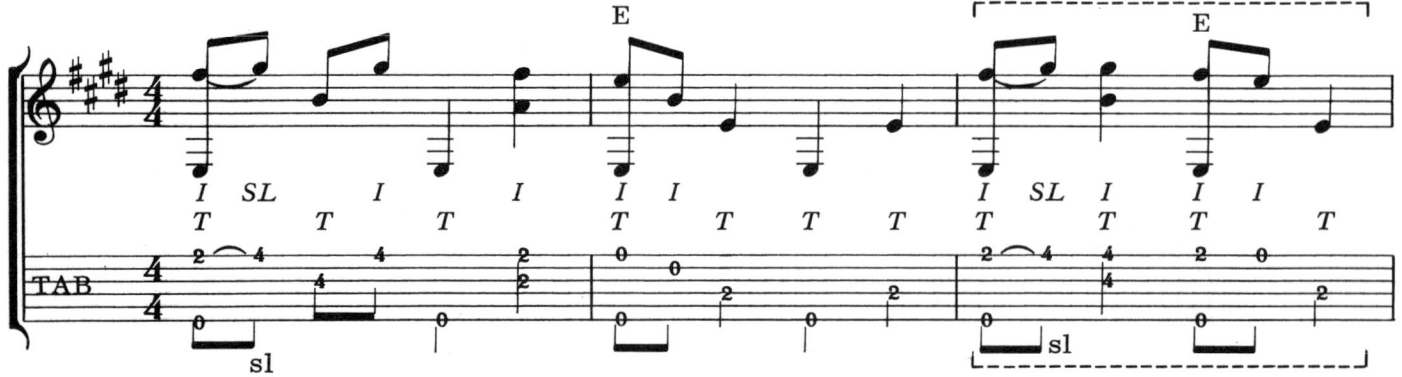

See See Rider-Solo

See See Rider-Melody

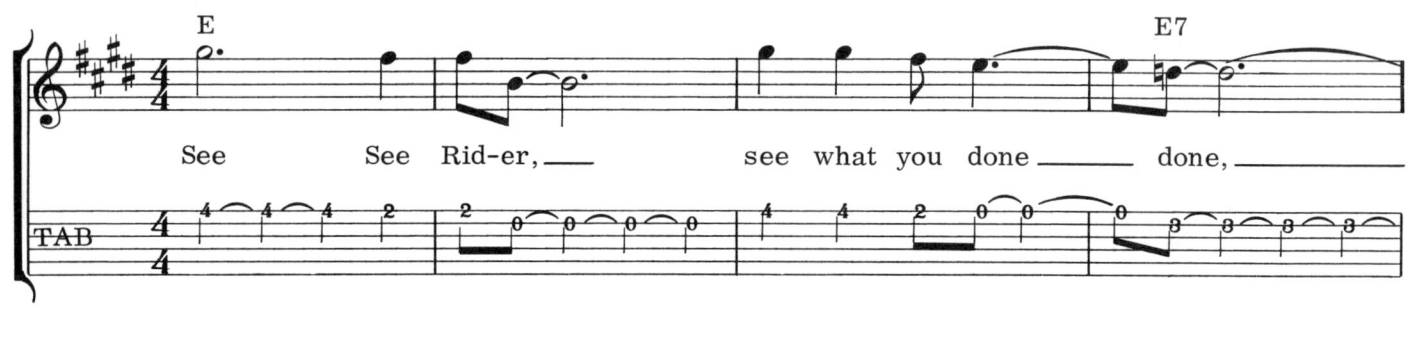
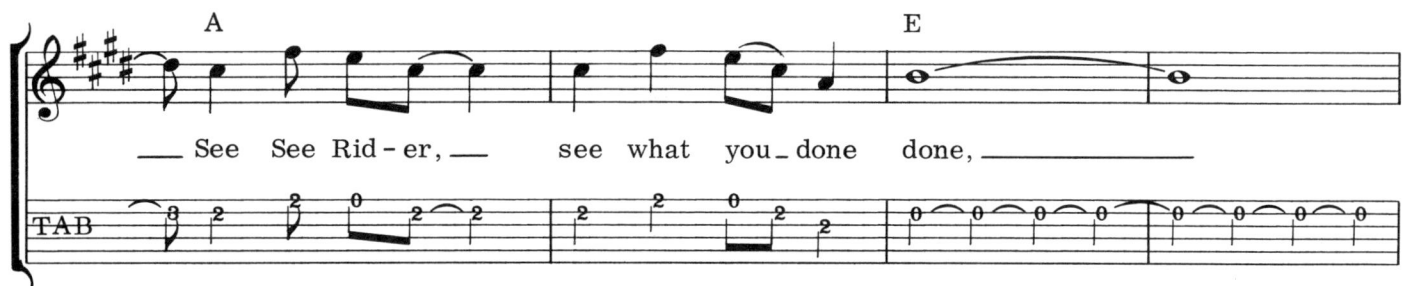

I wish I was a catfish, swimmin' in the sea, (3x)
I'd swim over there, and bring my baby back to me.

I'm goin' away, baby, won't be back till fall, (3x)
And if I find me a good woman, I won't be back at all.

Make me your sidetrack, till your mainline come, (3x)
I'll do you as good as your mainline ever done.

THREE-FINGER PICKING

The use of three fingers for fingerpicking is becoming increasingly popular among younger musicians. The use of the middle finger in addition to the index finger and thumb does not necessarily enable you to play more notes, but it does allow the fingers additional relaxation and results in a more even sound. The thumb, however, must do the same work in both two and three-finger picking.

The best way to begin three-finger picking is to go back to the beginning of this book and replay all the songs that we have learned using the middle finger instead of the index finger to pick the melody notes. This may seem difficult at first but you will find that in learning fingerpicking we have not been simply training our fingers, we have been learning a form of coordination which is easily transferrable to the middle finger. As soon as your middle finger feels comfortable playing melody, you are ready to begin this chapter.

In both the music and the tablature, the index finger will again be represented by the letter "I" and the middle finger by the letter "M."

OH, MARY DON'T YOU WEEP — THREE-FINGER PICKING

Three-finger picking allows the melody notes to be distributed between the index and middle fingers of the right hand. This is done in a very special way. By carefully inspecting the music to *Oh, Mary, Don't You Weep*, you will see that there are two basic right-hand positions in this song. For the first four measures the right hand is positioned so that the middle finger picks the first string and the index finger picks the second string. Notice that *all* the notes on the first string are picked by the middle finger and *all* the notes on the second string are picked by the index finger.

The second right-hand position is used in the 5th measure of this song. The fingers of the right hand have been moved down one string so that the index finger is now picking the third string and the middle finger is now picking the second string.

Oh, Mary, Don't You Weep - Melody

Mary wore three links of chain,
Every link was Jesus' name,
Pharoah's army got drownded
Oh, Mary, don't you weep.

Mary wore three links of chain,
Every link was Freedom's name,
Pharoah's army got drownded,
Oh, Mary, don't you weep.

One of these nights about twelve o'clock,
This old world is gonna reel and rock,
Pharoah's army got drownded,
Oh, Mary, don't you weep.

Moses stood on the Red Sea shore,
Smotin' the water with a two-by-four,
Pharoah's army got drownded
Oh, Mary, don't you weep.

God gave Noah the rainbow sign,
No more water but the fire next time.
Pharoah's army got drownded,
Oh, Mary, don't you weep.

HUSH LITTLE BABY — NEW RIGHT-HAND POSITION

This song will give further practice in changing right-hand positions. In addition, a new right-hand position is used in the 1st measure. Here the index finger must pick the *third* string and the middle finger must pick the *first* string.

Hush, Little Baby-Solo

Hush, Little Baby-Melody

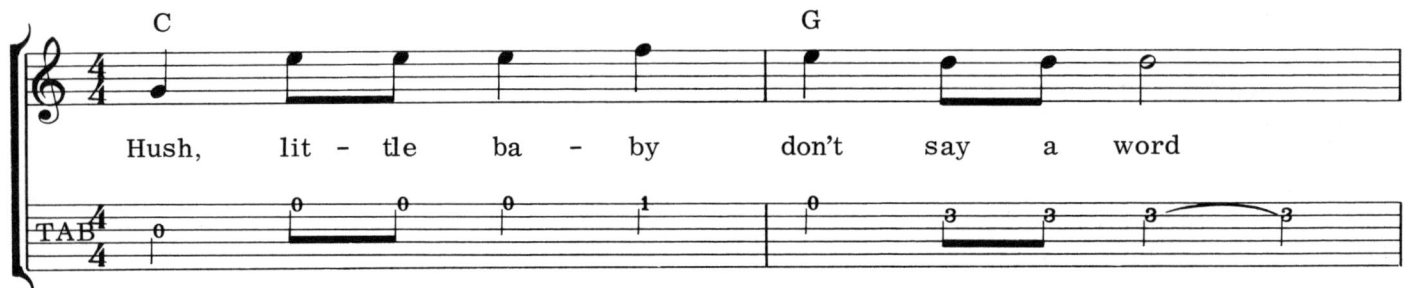

And if that mocking bird don't sing,
Poppa's gonna buy you a diamond ring.

And if that diamond ring turns brass,
Poppa's gonna buy you a looking glass.

And if that looking glass is broke,
Poppa's gonna buy you a billy goat.

And if that billy goat don't pull,
Poppa's gonna buy you a cart and bull.

And if that cart and bull turn over,
Poppa's gonna buy you a dog named Rover.

And if that dog named Rover won't bark,
Poppa's gonna buy you a horse and cart.

And if that horse and cart fall down,
You're still the sweetest little baby in town.

RAILROAD BILL #3 — HAMMERS

This version of *Railroad Bill* will give us an opportunity to integrate the off-beat hammer into three-finger picking. Be very careful to observe which fingers of the right hand are used in each measure. Some of them are tricky.

Railroad Bill 3-Solo

OH, MARY, DON'T YOU WEEP #2 — HAMMERS AND PICKS

The complexity of this arrangement of *Oh, Mary, Don't You Weep* is greater than the version which began this chapter. Compare the two versions to see how the various ornamental techniques are used. Off-beat hammers are used in the 1st and 5th measures. The on-beat pick in the 4th measure may cause some difficulty, therefore it has been outlined in the Chord Analysis Box.

CHORD ANALYSIS BOX — OH MARY, DON'T YOU WEEP #2 (measures 3-4)

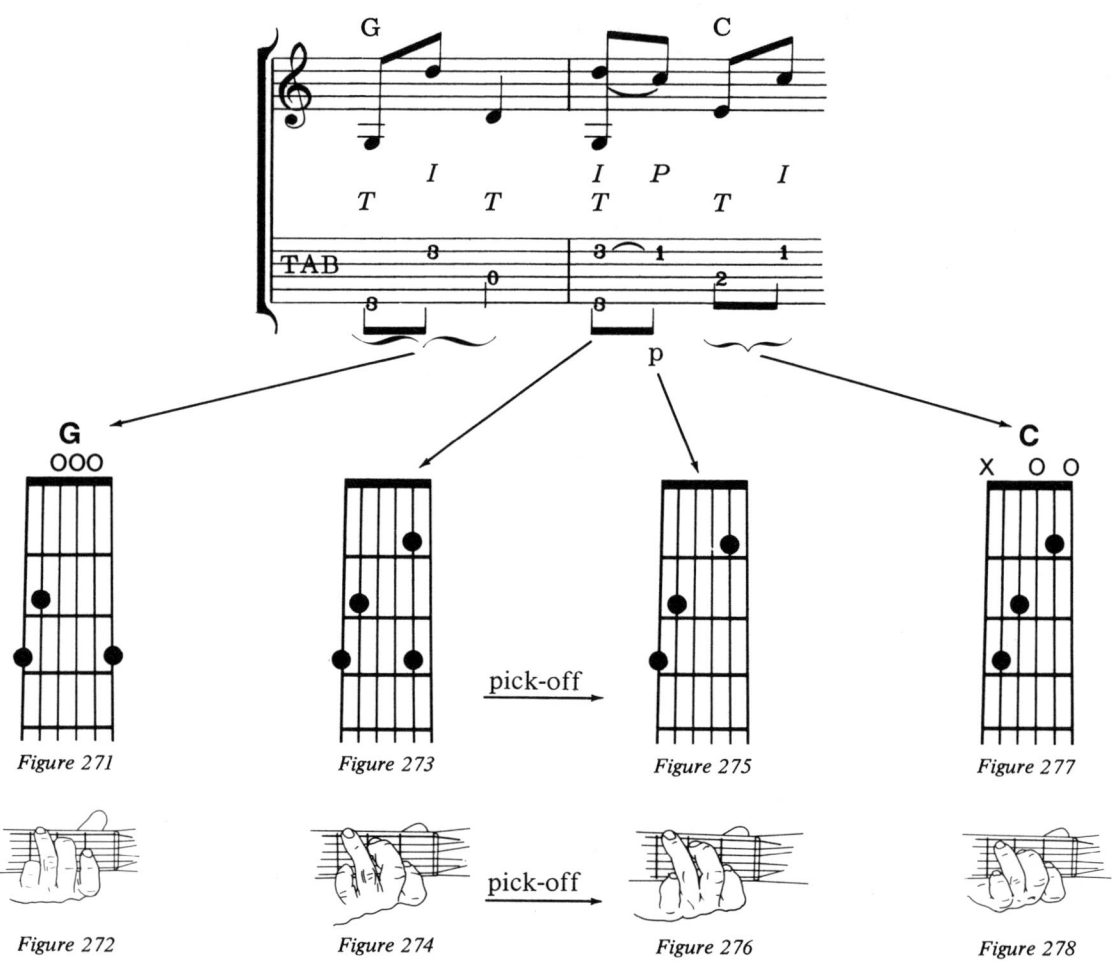

Figure 271

Figure 272

Figure 273

Figure 274

pick-off

Figure 275

Figure 276

Figure 277

Figure 278

Oh, Mary, Don't You Weep 2 - Solo

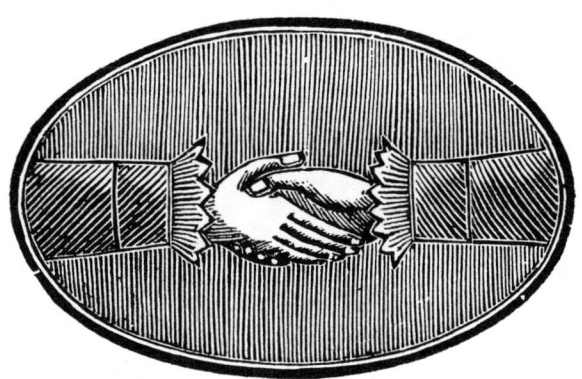

CASEY JONES – KEY OF G

This is an interesting three-finger version of a famous fingerpicking tune. The only difficulty that may be encountered in this song is in the 7th measure. This is explained in the Chord Analysis Box.

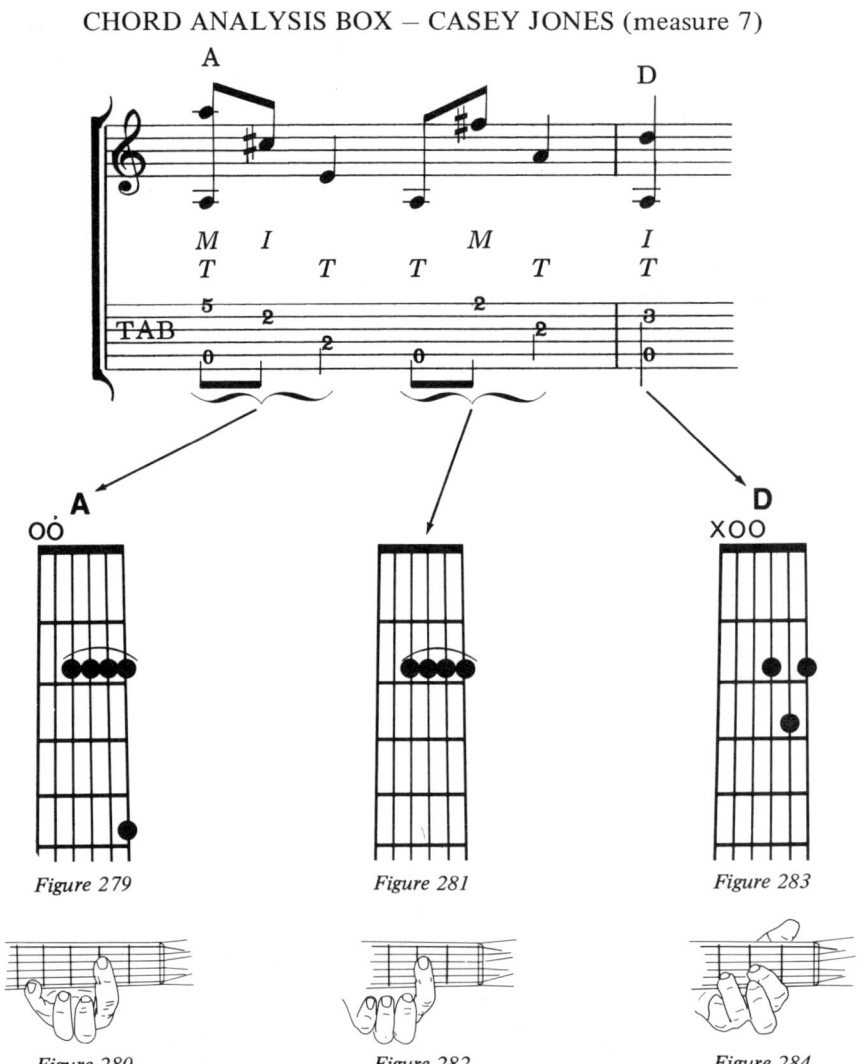

CHORD ANALYSIS BOX – CASEY JONES (measure 7)

Figure 279

Figure 280

Figure 281

Figure 282

Figure 283

Figure 284

Casey Jones-Solo

FRANKIE AND JOHNNY — KEY OF A

Frankie and Johnny is a slow song. It is often more difficult to fingerpick a slow song since any rhythmic irregularities can be easily heard.

Frankie and Johnny-Solo

Frankie and Johnny-Melody

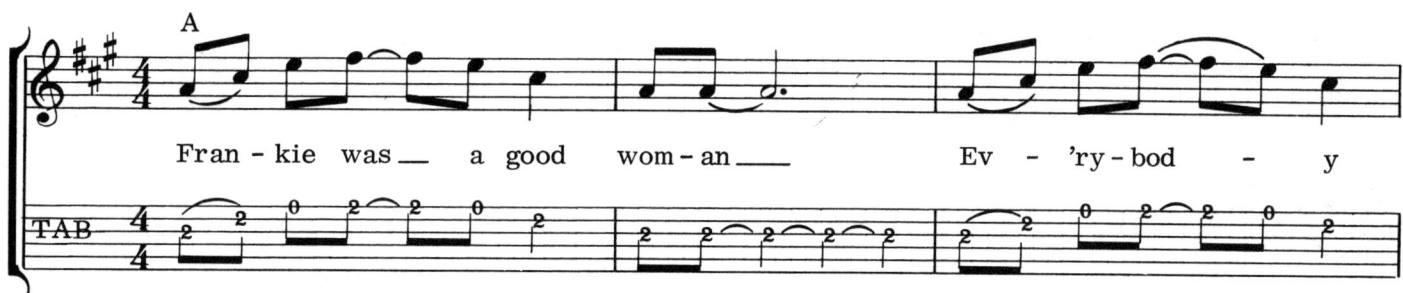

Frankie was a good woman,
Everybody knows,
She gave her Johnny a hundred dollars
And he spent it on them whores,
He was her man, but he done her wrong.

Frankie went down to the bar-room,
Asked for a glass of beer,
She said to the lovin' bartender,
"Has my lovin' Johnny been here?
"He was my man, but he's doin' me wrong."

Says, "Frankie, I'll tell you no story,
"Frankie, I'll tell you no lie,
"I saw your man about an hour ago
"With a girl named Alice Fry,
"He was your man, but he's doin' you wrong."

Frankie went back to the crib house,
This time it weren't for fun,
Under her silk kimono
She brought her other man's gun,
To kill her man, 'cause he done her wrong.

Frankie went down to the coke joint,
She stood and rung the bell,
Says, "If I find my man in here,
"I'll kill him sure as hell,
"He was my man, but he's doin' me wrong."

Frankie pulled out her gun,
She squeezed that old forty-four,
That old gun went rooty-toot-toot,
And Johnny rolled on the floor,
He was her man, but he done her wrong.

"Roll me over Frankie,
"Roll me over slow,
"Roll me on my right side,
"Cause my left side hurts me so,
"I was her man, but I done her wrong."

Roll out your rubber-tired carriage,
Roll out your rubber-tired hacks,
There's twelve men goin' to the graveyard
and eleven comin' back,
He was her man, but he done her wrong.

SUGAR BABE — MORE HAMMERS

This song involves some rather complicated left hand hammers. Work through the song slowly and you will have no difficulty with these complex techniques.

Sugar Babe - Solo

MIDNIGHT SPECIAL – COMPLEX THREE-FINGER PICKING

This is the most difficult song in this book so be very patient in learning it. In the solo up to four notes must be picked consecutively on the same string. The method of picking these notes is to alternate the middle and index fingers in a manner familiar to classical and flamenco guitarists. However, many traditional folk guitarists use only one finger to pick consecutive notes. Try both methods and decide which is easier for you.

CHORD ANALYSIS BOX – MIDNIGHT SPECIAL (measure 7)

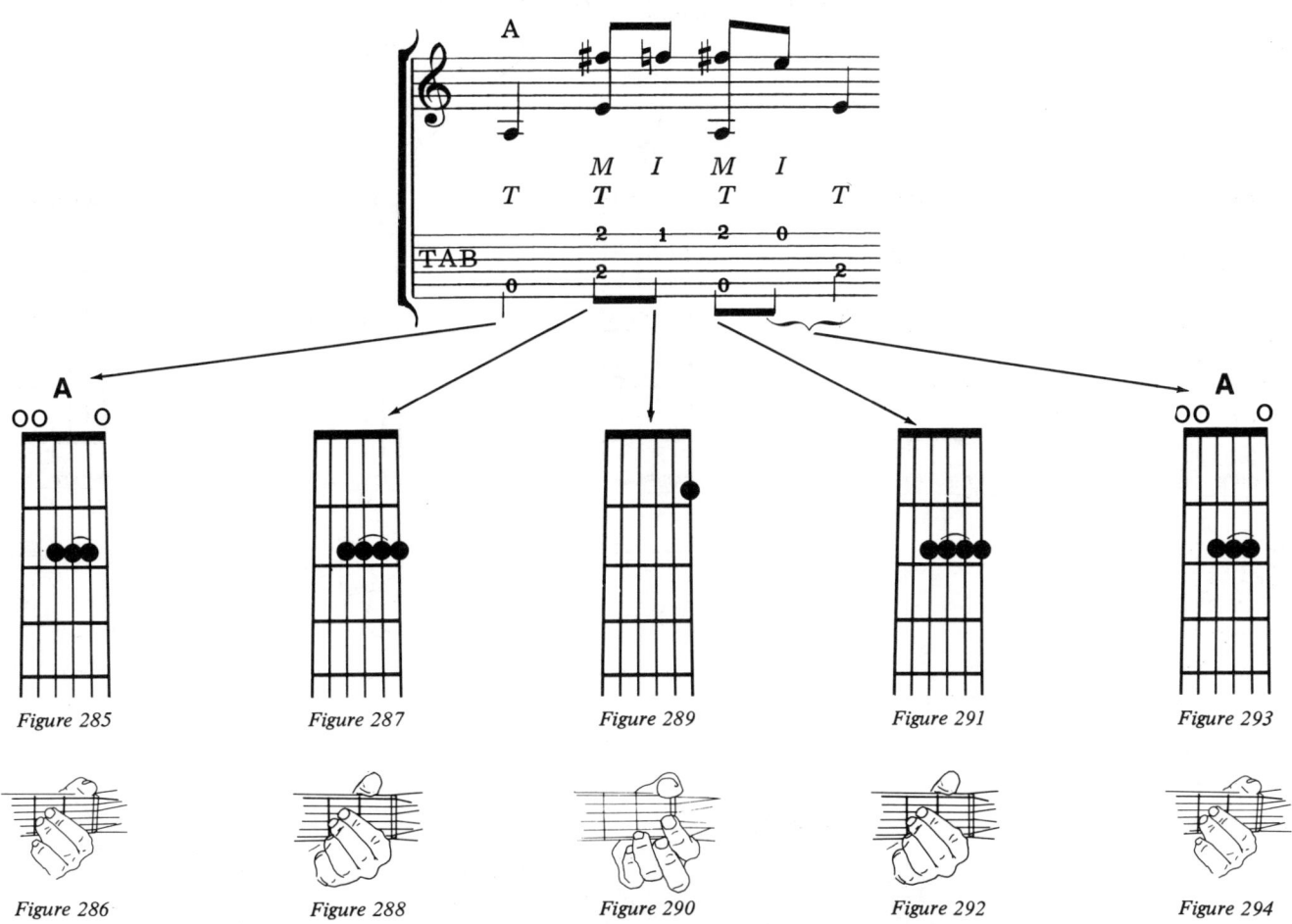

Figure 285

Figure 286

Figure 287

Figure 288

Figure 289

Figure 290

Figure 291

Figure 292

Figure 293

Figure 294

CHORD ANALYSIS BOX – MIDNIGHT SPECIAL (measures 8-9)

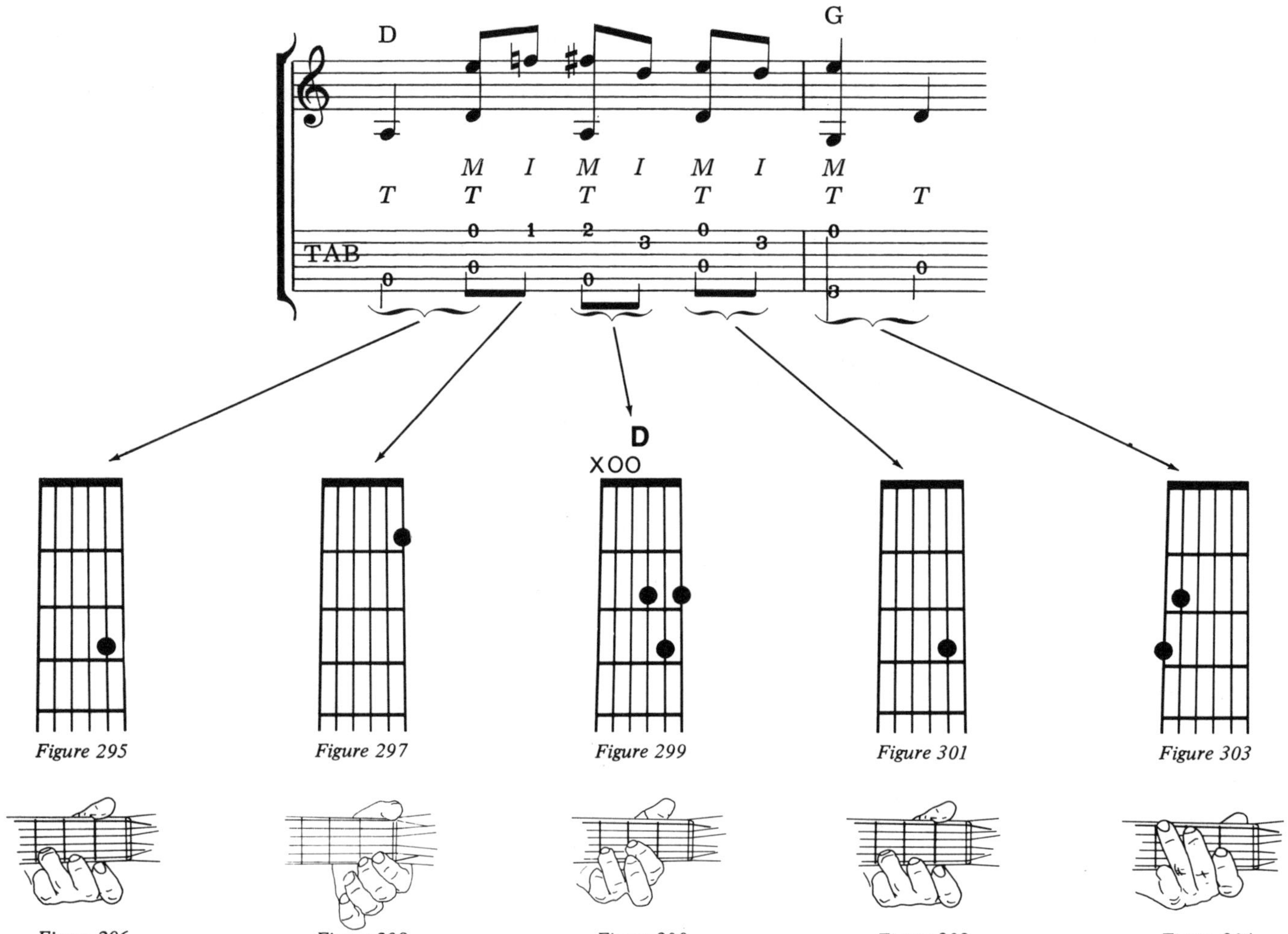

Figure 295

Figure 296

Figure 297

Figure 298

Figure 299

Figure 300

Figure 301

Figure 302

Figure 303

Figure 304

Midnight Special-Solo

Midnight Special-Melody

112

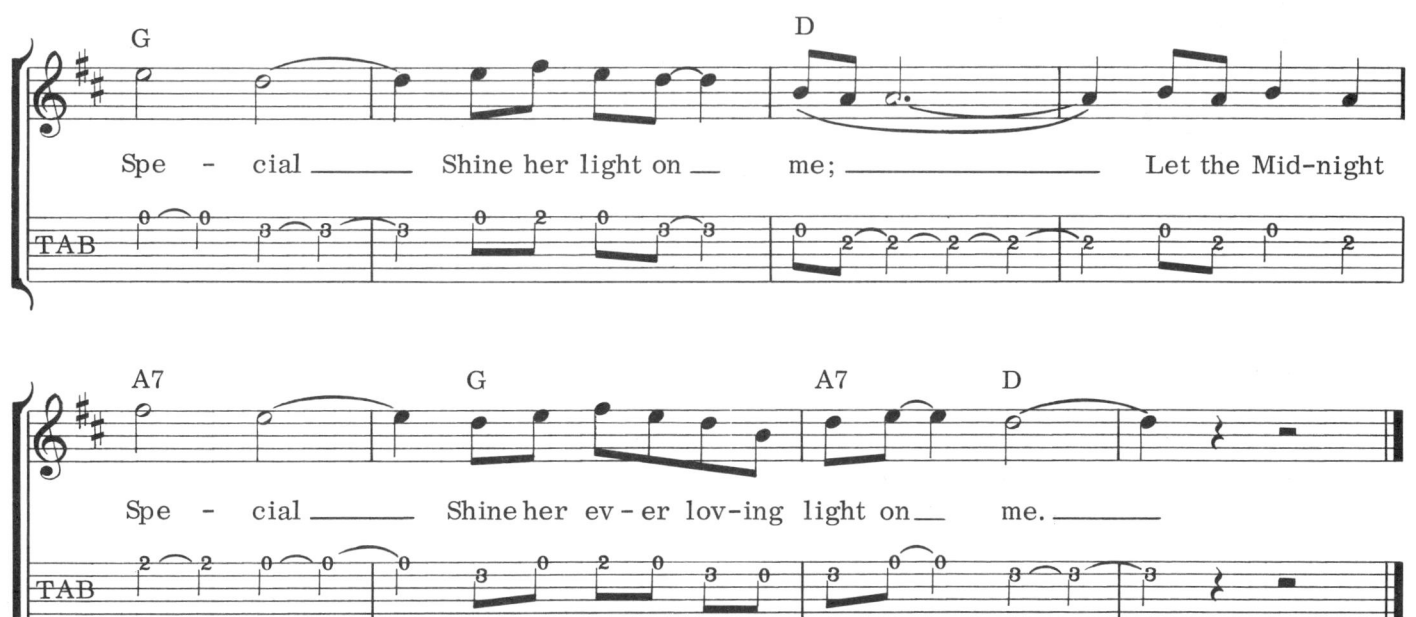

If you go to Houston,
You better walk right;
You better not stagger,
You better not fight;
Sheriff Benson will arrest you,
He'll take you on down,
And if the jury finds you guilty,
Your penitentiary bound.

Yonder comes Miss Rosey,
How'n the world do you know?
You can tell by her apron,
And the dress she wore;
Umbrella on her shoulder,
Piece o' paper in her hand,
She gonna tell the Captain,
"I want my man."

DOING IT ALL YOURSELF

In this chapter there are a dozen songs written in both music and tablature in the keys we have studied. Your task is to arrange these songs using the fingerpicking styles we have learned. In addition, they will give you an opportunity to use the various forms of ornamentation that have been illustrated such as hammers, picks, and slides. Technical assistance is given in the form of footnotes. This chapter will test how well you have learned the material.

Bury Me Beneath the Willow-Melody

Chorus:

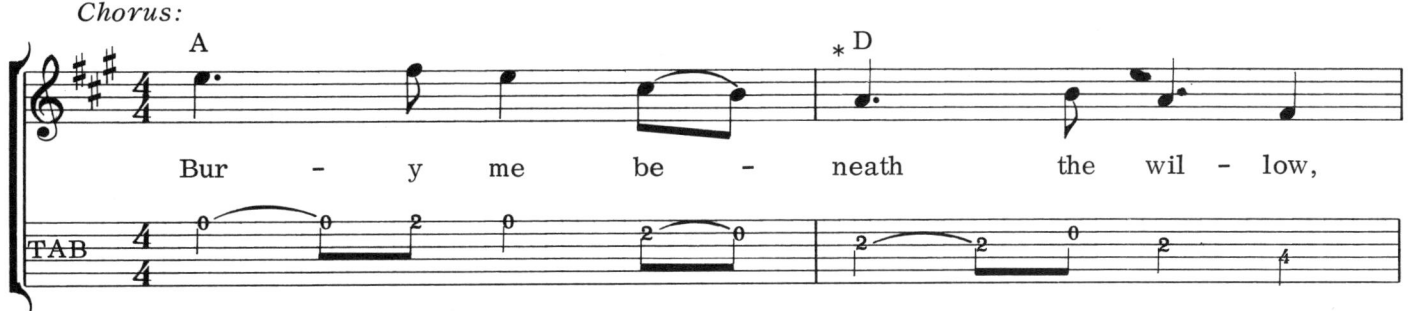

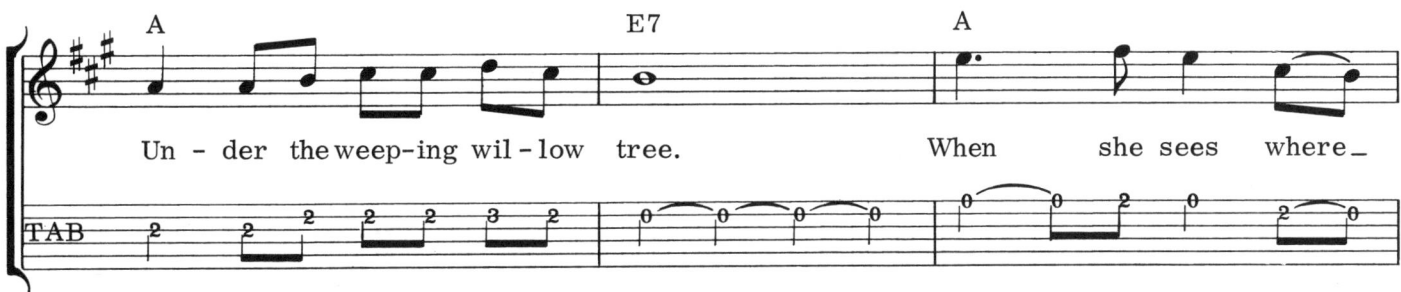

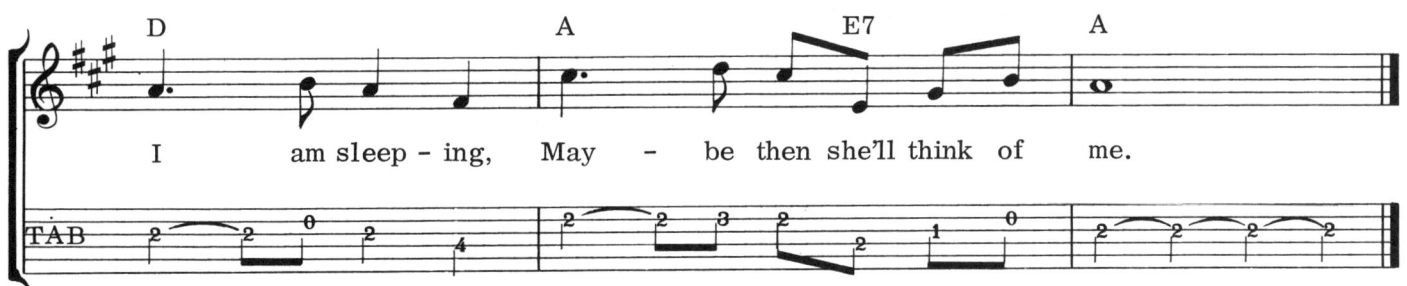

*See Figures 59 thru 62.

(Sung to tune of chorus)
Tomorrow was to be our wedding,
Where, oh, where can she be?
She's gone, she's gone to love another;
She no longer cares for me.

My heart is sad, and I am lonely,
Thinking of the one I love.
Will I meet her, oh, no, never,
Till we meet in heaven above.

She told me that she loved me dearly,
How could I believe her untrue?
Till an angel whispered softly,
She's been untrue to you.

The Girl on the Greenbriar Shore—Melody

'Twas in the year of ninety two, In the merry month of

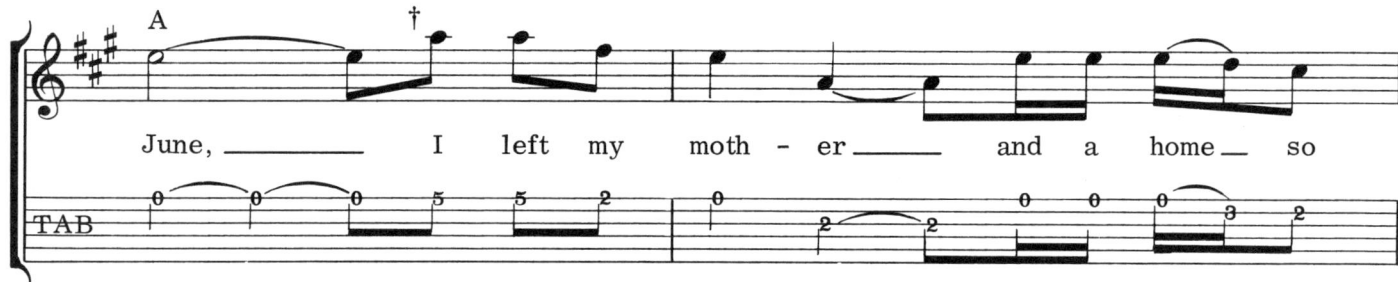

June, I left my mother and a home so

dear For the girl I loved on the Green-briar Shore.

*See Figures 93 and 94.
†See Figures 73 thru 78.

My mother dear, she said to me
"Oh, son, oh son, don't go,
"Don't leave your mother and a home so dear
"For that girl on the Greenbriar shore."

But I was young and reckless, too,
And I craved a reckless life;
I left my mother with a broken heart,
And I took that girl to be my wife.

Her hair was dark and curly, too,
And her loving eyes were blue;
Her cheeks were like the red, red rose,
That girl I loved on the Greenbriar shore.

The years rolled by and the months rolled on,
She left me all alone;
Now I remember what my mother said,
"Never trust a girl on the Greenbriar shore."

Handsome Molly-Melody

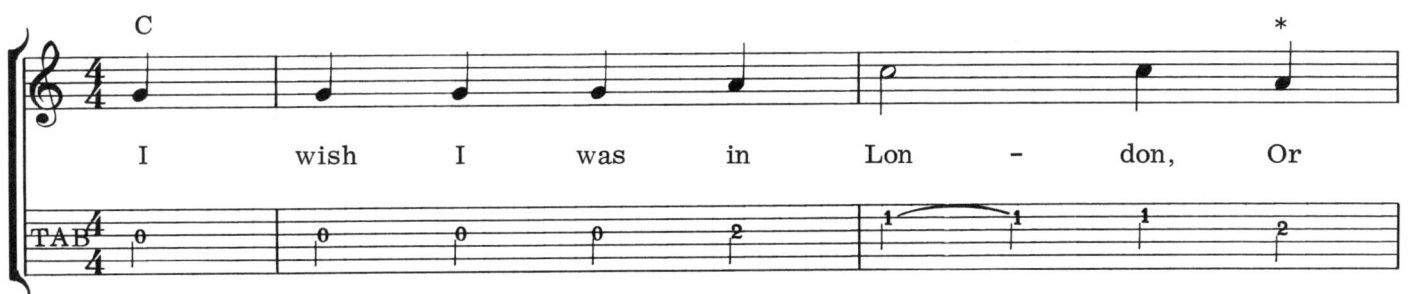

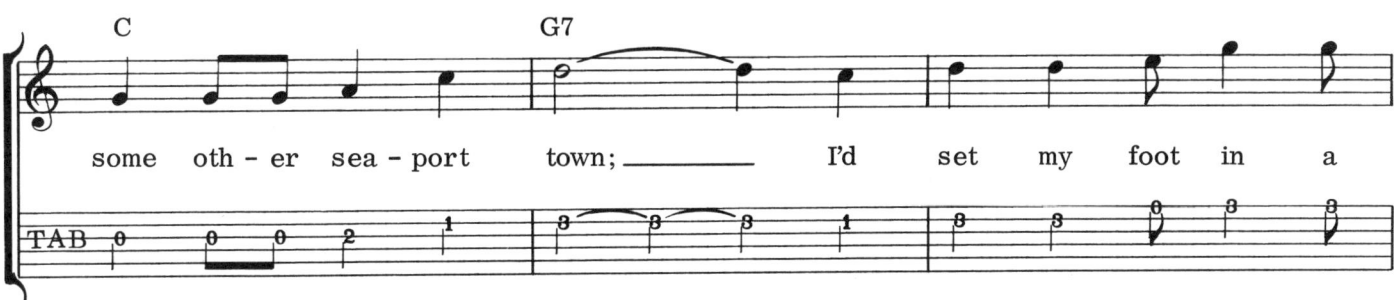

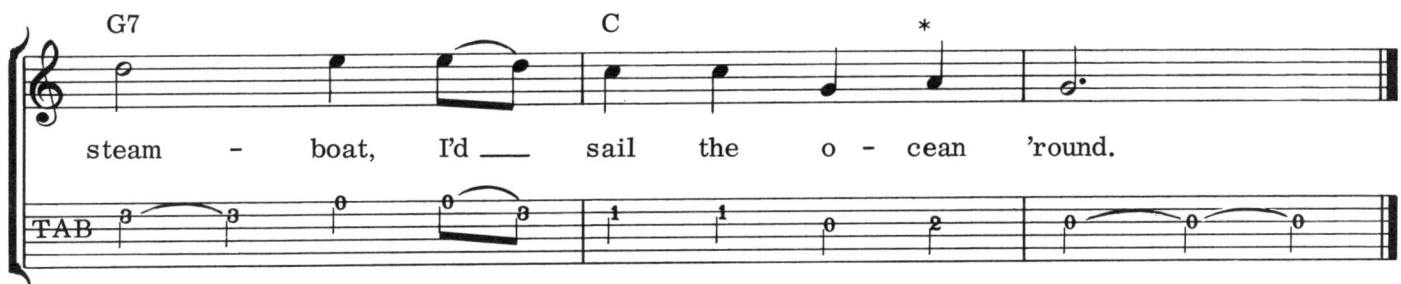

*Use hammer as in Figures 173 thru 178.

While sailing around the ocean,
While sailing 'round the sea,
I'd think of handsome Molly
Wherever she may be.

You rode to church last Sunday,
You passed me on by;
I know your mind is changin'
By the rovin' of your eye.

Don't you remember, Molly,
When you gave me your right hand?
Said if you ever married,
Then I would be the man.

Now you've broke your promise, Molly,
Go home with whom you please,
While my poor heart is breakin'
You're lying at your ease.

Her hair was black as a raven,
Her eyes as black as coal,
Her cheeks was like lilies
Out in the morning cold.

Oh, Babe, It Ain't No Lie-Melody

Been all 'round this whole world,
Lord, I just got back today,
Work all the week, hon', and give it all to you,
Honey, babe, what more can I do?

East Virginia Blues-Melody

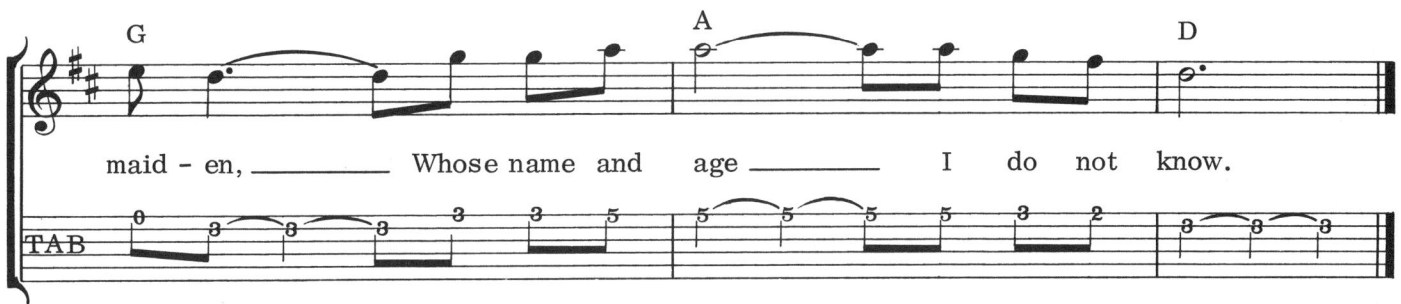

*See Figures 89 thru 94
**See Figures 71 and 72.
†See Figures 87 and 88.
††See Figures 245 thru 248.

Her hair was dark in color,
And her cheeks were rosy red;
And on her breast, she wore white lilies
Where I long to lay my head.

Papa says we cannot marry;
Mama says you'll never do;
If you ever learn to love me
I will run away with you.

I'd rather be in some dark hollow,
Where the sun would never shine,
Than to see you with another,
And to know that you'd never be mine.

I don't want your greenback dollars,
I don't want your watch and chain,
All I want is your heart, darlin',
Say that you'll be mine again.

Tom Cat Blues—Melody

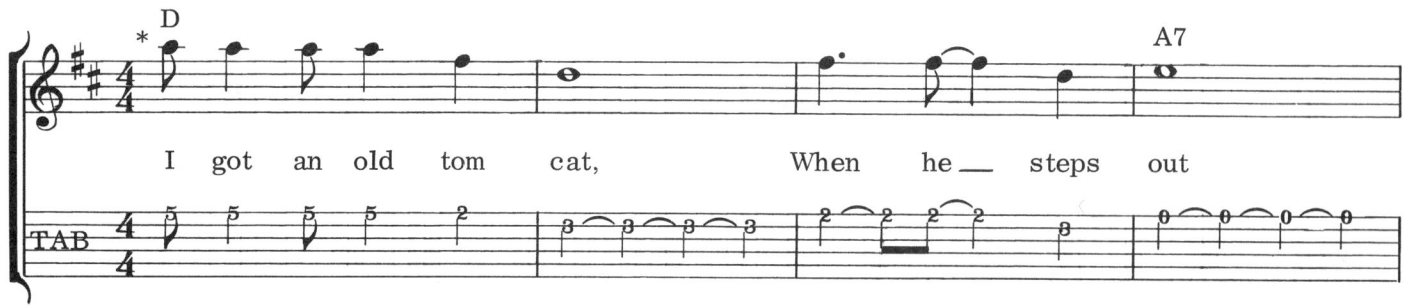

*See Figures 89 thru 94.

"Here comes Ring Tail Tom,
"He's boss around the town,
"And if you got your heat turned up,
"Better turn your damper down."

Ring Tail Tom on the fence,
The old pussycat on the ground,
Ring Tail Tom come off of that fence,
And they went round and round.

Lord he's quick on the trigger,
He's a natural-born crack shot,
He got a new target every night,
And he sure does practice a lot.

He makes them roust about
He makes them roll their eyes,
They just can't resist my Ring Tail Tom,
No matter how hard they tries.

You better watch old Ring Tail Tom,
He's running 'round this town,
He won't have no pussycats
Come a-tomcattin' around.

Nine-Pound Hammer-Melody

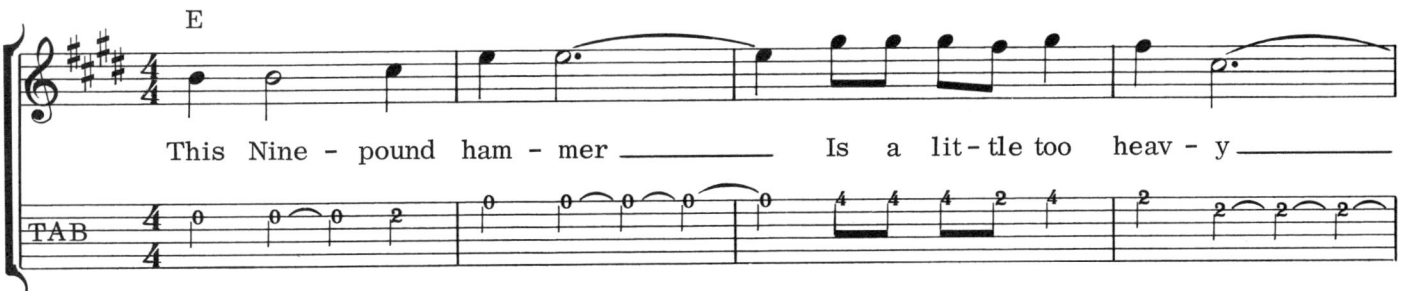

There ain't a hammer
In this tunnel,
That rings like mine,
That rings like mine.

It's a long way to Harlan,
It's a long way to Hazard,
For a little booze,
For a little booze.

This here hammer,
It killed John Henry,
But it can't kill me,
But it can't kill me.

Now, John Henry,
He left his hammer,
Painted in red,
Painted in red.

Just A Closer Walk With Thee - Melody

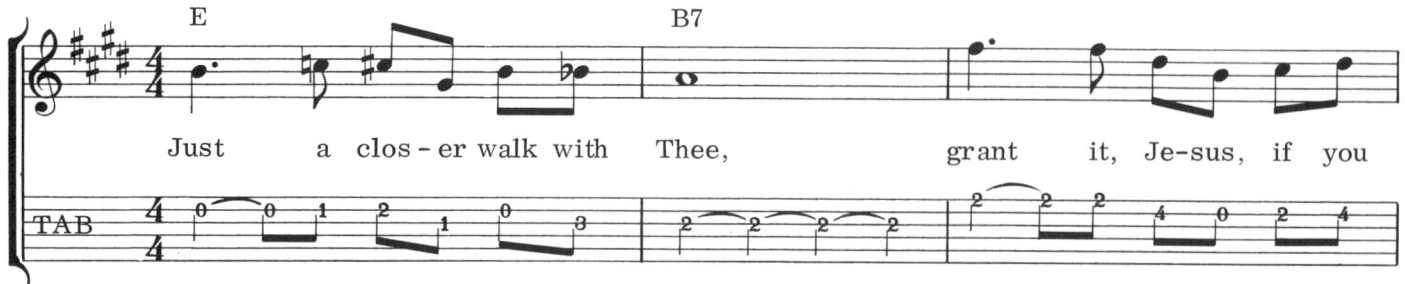

Just a clos-er walk with Thee, grant it, Je-sus, if you

please.___ Dai - ly, walk-ing close to

Thee, Let it be, dear Lord, Let it be.

Through the days of toil that's near,
If I fall, dear Lord, who cares;
Who with me my burden shares?
None but Thee, dear Lord, none but Thee.

When my feeble life is o'er,
Time for me will be no more;
Guide me gently, safely on,
To Thy shore, dear Lord, to Thy shore.

Camptown Races-Melody

Swanee River - Melody

*See Figures 89 thru 94.
**Use pick similar to hammer in Figures 179 thru 182.

Sinner Man-Melody

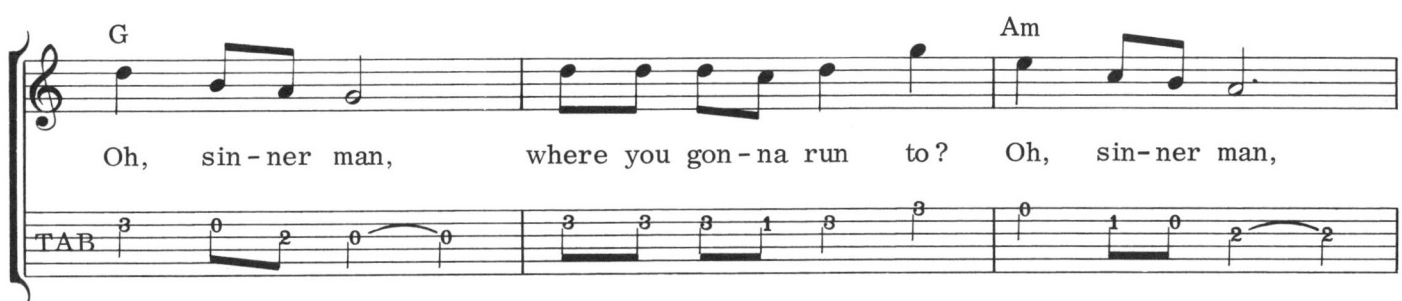

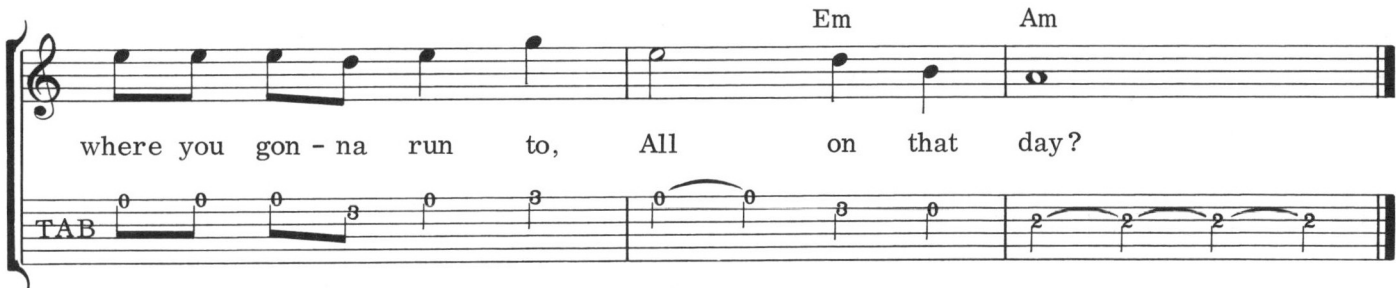

Run to the rock, the rock was a-melting, (3x)
All on that day.

Run to the sea, the sea was a-boiling, (3x)
All on that day.

Run to the moon, the moon was a-bleeding, (3x)
All on that day.

Run to the Lord, Lord, won't you hide me? (3x)
All on that Day.

Run to the Devil, Devil was a-waiting, (3x)
All on that day.

Keep Your Lamp Trimmed and Burning-Melody